TELLING STORIES

JOHN BROUGHAN

Publisher's Information

EBookBakery Books

Author contact: tellingstories2018@gmail.com

ISBN 978-1-938517-86-0

© 2018 by John Broughan

There are only two ways
to live your life.

One is though
nothing is a miracle.

The other is as if
everything is.

ALBERT EINSTEIN

Collage of early years

CONTENTS

INTRODUCTION

I am born.

(OK, I realize it's a three word sentence and I am already guilty of plagiarism, and from a work of the great Charles Dickens, no less! But I could not help myself. Ever since reading Dickens's *David Copperfield,* I decided that if I ever wrote my memoir this would have to be my first sentence.)

To be honest, I do not remember much of that day, or, indeed, much of anything of my early years – other than crawling in our Grove Street living room with a hairpin I found on the floor which I assumed went into the electric plug on the nearby wall. Once airborne and thrown against the opposite wall, I clearly noted to my infant self, never make that mistake again. In fact, it made such an impression on me that, seventy years later, I still fear changing light bulbs while secretly admiring all the courageous electricians. Therefore, my life stories actually start when I was six year old and off to first grade.

With my admission of plagiarism out of the way, I can now confidently disclose that the rest of the words are unquestionably mine – the good, the bad and the ugly. My goal throughout is simply to inform while entertaining my family and good friends with whom I wish to share this "literary achievement," more than five years in the making. For this reason, my stories are not about my family, but for my children, their spouses and the beautiful grandchildren they have provided us.

Finally, this memoir would not exist (or if it did, it would be a total mess) if it were not for my typist and exceptional editor – who also shared many of these life experiences for the last half-century. The added value that she likes to cook and shovel snow makes her the perfect spouse. Our own children would also say she was a good mother as well as a special Gigi to each of the grandchildren.

Thank you for taking the time to join me on my life's journey. I hope you enjoy reading these ruminations as much as I did writing them.

SUGAR

"JUST SAY THANK YOU," my father whispered in my ear. "A simple thank you would be fine, but you need to say something."

But nothing came out! There I stood like a thankless mute statue. For the first and likely last time in my life, I was speechless. This, in spite of the thank you comments I had carefully prepared in anticipation of the first milestone event in my life. As I stared straight ahead at the hundreds of eyes totally focused on me, my mind was blank and my tongue was firmly locked inside my sealed lips. Standing directly below me in the orchestra pit stood a huge real live horse – my horse!

It started two months earlier at the beginning of summer. I was excited about finally entering first grade at Holy Trinity School in a few months. One afternoon my mother's friend, Betty Gardner, was visiting, as she did most days of the week after finishing her job at the Greenfield *Recorder*.

"Can you believe the Garden Theater is giving away a horse next month?"

"Where did you hear that?" my mother asked.

"I read it while working on the paper today. It seems they are promoting their new "cool air" system so people will go to the movies when it is hot this summer."

I listened intently as she went on to explain that every time someone went to the Garden Theater during the next month they would have a chance to vote for someone to win the horse.

Later that evening, with a plan of action and my mind made up that I was going to own a horse, I went into the den to bother my father as he read the *Recorder* and enjoyed his martini.

"I want to win the horse the Garden is giving away," I announced.

"And how do you plan to do that?"

"I'll just go around town and ask everyone to vote for me."

"That's a good idea, but I'm afraid people going to the movies will probably vote for themselves or one of their friends," he patiently explained.

Commencing a lifetime of never heeding perfectly sound logic or reason, I left the room now confident I would soon be the proud owner of my very own "Trigger."

The following day I walked around the neighborhood and asked everyone I saw to vote for me. Buoyed by the smiles and acceptance I received, I took the next important step to realize my goal.

Our telephone was in the hall, and I had recently learned how to dial the five numbers needed to call a friend. Next to the rotary phone was my mother's directory. It was a six inch long steel case with the letters of the alphabet running down the right side. There was an arrow you could move to any letter, and when you hit the bottom button, the case flipped open to the names and phone numbers of relatives and friends. I had always found it fun to play with; now it was my key to victory.

Using my secret formula of "random selection," I started dialing the listed numbers.

"Hi, I am Jack Broughan. Will you vote for me to win the horse when you go to the movies?"

"Are you Tom or John's son?" I was asked.

"I think John. Tom is my uncle."

"Sure, I'll vote for you. In fact, my wife and I are going to the Garden Saturday night."

I was off to the races! I went from letter to letter on that magic directory, gaining confidence with each and every call. Everyone said yes, and thanked me for calling them. I did have a challenge to overcome, however. We were on a party line with three neighbors, so I was not able to use the phone all the time. Soon this minor setback became a benefit. Since everyone on the line always listened in on each other's calls, my neighbors became aware of my mission, and they in turn started to call their friends and ask them to vote for me. Little did I realize, at the time, that I had perhaps started the first telemarketing campaign in the history of the town of Greenfield.

And it worked!

"I can't quite believe it," I heard my father tell our entire family later that summer, "but Jack has actually won the horse." To say I was excited was an understatement.

My father then explained how we would all go to the Garden Theater the next Saturday where I would be given the horse between the double feature movies. That very evening I started to prepare for the little speech my father told me I should make when accepting my new prized possession.

By Saturday I was ready. I would explain how I had always wanted my own horse, ever since I was a small child, and especially after petting the milkman's horse when he delivered our milk bottles. I would further elaborate on how I loved Trigger after seeing my first Roy Roger's movie at that very same Garden Theater last year. And there was more. (Anyone who has ever read my essays or heard me make a presentation later in my career would not be surprised at such an ample abundance of my scintillating verbiage.)

With great excitement, my parents and I arrived at the Garden Theater Saturday evening. Now you need to know that, for me, the Garden was the most magical place in the whole world. Not only was the stage and screen huge, it also had a large orchestra pit and an even larger balcony. Most importantly, when the lights dimmed the ceiling came alive with twinkling stars and beautiful white clouds moving across that ceiling sky. I loved going to the Garden. That Saturday night I saw it from a completely different angle. As the lights went on following the first film, my father and I, together with the theater manager, walked out on to an incredibly bright stage. I peered out at the totally full theater. In the audience were many who had voted for me, and now were awaiting my every word.

You already know the rest of the story. Following that night of humiliation, my father took me to the horse barn and corral at the end of Main Street owned by his friend, Joe. He had agreed to temporarily house my horse as a favor to my father. I petted my new friend, and Joe put me on the horse's back so together we could walk proudly around that small corral. I was the happiest guy in the whole world.

That weekend my parents and I took the train to Brooklyn to visit my grandmother. On the way home, we had dinner in the train's dining car. While playing with the cubes of sugar in the bowl on the table (as children inevitably do), I asked my father if horses liked sugar.

"Yes, I believe they are quite fond of sweet things," he assured me.

As I immediately scooped a bunch of cubes into my pocket, I announced "I am going to call my horse Sugar."

After our return to Greenfield, the family went to Joe's so I could feed Sugar his new treats and advise him of his new name. As I petted him goodbye, little did I know that I would never see him again.

A few days later my father came home and told me that he sold Sugar to a family that had a large farm with a barn outside of town. He said he used the money from the sale to buy me a new swing set, with a slide, for our back yard. I immediately went into a raging tantrum; worthy of any wronged seven year old, and threatened to never talk to my father again. More importantly, I vowed I would never share the swing set with my younger sisters.

The swing set arrived and my mood mellowed, although I still pushed my sisters off whenever they tried to get on "my swings." Soon after, summer vacation was over and I went off to first grade.

Quickly, Sugar became a distant memory - one that featured my first exciting victory, marred by my humbling failure to properly thank those who made it possible.

Hopefully, they have forgiven me.

The Winner and His Horse

It Was Elementary – "The Book Ends"

AS I CAUTIOUSLY STEPPED into my first grade classroom that warm September morning, I looked straight up for a view of my teacher. She was so tall and almost completely covered in a strange black and white costume.

She seemed taller than any woman I had ever seen, probably due to some kind of black square small tower on top of her head. It even covered part of her face and then continued down her entire body almost covering her black shoes that looked like they belonged on an old lady. She had gigantic Rosary beads around her waist that almost touched her shoes. A white triangle covered half her forehead, and a hard white bib was tucked under her chin that looked like a huge paper plate. Even more frightening, her entire body was covered except for part of her face and her hands. Those hands seemed so clean. I always wondered how she was able to make them so clean – and stay that way all day.

Her name was Sister Agnes Angela. My mother explained to me that it was a special name she had chosen when she had given herself to God. "All the nuns at Holy Trinity wear that special habit, or God's dress, and because of their vocation, when they are not teaching, they are praying in the large house next to the school."

What little of her face we could see was quite pretty. She seemed very kind, and I immediately liked her, in spite of her height. Once I and my classmates were assigned our own desks, I began to think that I would like going to school.

Sister Agnes Angela did make it fun while teaching us lots of new things. First, we learned numbers and then letters. Later on, she taught us how to write those letters that had been discovered by some guy called Palmer. But the best part of class that year was learning all about the adventures of Dick, Jane and Spot. Boy, did those three have a lot of fun! I must have done quite well under the tutelage of Agnes Angela, as my mother saved every paper I brought home – most with stars on them. (I should note that she actually gave them to me in a large box as a wedding gift twenty years later. The box also included second grade, third, fourth... Well, you get the idea. She was quite the saver, and I was the first child!)

As the year went along, I became quite comfortable and felt secure in that first grade classroom. I really had no desire to move on to second grade unless Sister Agnes Angela came too. Later in the year, when she taught us about saints, I believed she might be a candidate herself.

During recess I would often see the Sister who taught the other first grade, and she seemed crabby, and my friends in her class agreed with my observation. So each morning when we arrived in our classroom and said, "Good Morning, Sister" in unison, and then said our prayers, I would often say thank you to God for letting me have Sister Agnes Angela as my teacher.

All too quickly the year came to an end, and following summer vacation, I would be one step closer to the summit of Holy Trinity, eighth grade and graduation. As I climbed that grammar school ladder, I had other Sisters of every shape and size, all wearing that same habit. (As we got older we called the habits penguin suits, and would speculate what they actually looked like if they were not wearing them – would they even have any hair?)

While each Sister did her job, I can't remember the names of any, or tell you what they looked like. They were one big black blur. The one exception was my seventh grade teacher, Sister Mary Leona, a name I remember for all the wrong reasons. I did not like her, and she did not like me! Actually she did not like boys in general and thought their place was in the garment room adjacent to the classroom where she could slap us around for not paying attention or studying hard enough. I must admit I deserved my third trip to the garment room one day when she saw me sharing a piece of my creative artwork when I was supposedly doing an arithmetic assignment. The mistake was actually showing this work of art to my friend, Conrad Lanoue, sitting across the aisle. It was a drawing of Marilyn Monroe in a wedding dress flying through the air into the glove of Joe DiMaggio in center field of Yankee Stadium. While it was based on a current event, Sister Mary Leona did not find it amusing as she peered toward the back of the room to find us enjoying my masterpiece immensely.

A few weeks later I was not amused when she yelled at my friend and neighbor, Ann Lawler, for not answering correctly during a spelling bee. Ann had multiple sclerosis, and at that moment was having a seizure. As I ran over to help her, I wanted to smack Sister as I passed her, but even she felt guilty over this unfortunate act of meanness.

During that very long year with Sister Mary Leona I had seen one of the eighth grade teachers at recess and during sports after school. She was great fun and seemed as different from Mary Leona as night is from day. As importantly, unlike "Sister Mean," Rose Thomas really liked boys. Toward the end of seventh grade, in May, we wrote letters to the Blessed Mother to ask her to bless our parents and our sisters and brothers. I added a footnote: "Could I please be assigned to Sister Rose Thomas' eight grade class next year?" As we watched the letters burn in a large trash can with the ashes ascending directly to Mary, I really hoped she would get the message.

My prayer was answered, and in that final year at Holy Trinity, I found myself in the good hands of that very same Sister Rose Thomas. She was as short as Agnes Angela was tall (or perhaps she was not that short, we students were all much taller by then). She was not particularly attractive and had a distinguishing mole on her cheek, along with small hairs on her chin. She was firm and demanding in class, but I didn't mind, because she was warm, funny and fair.

During recess and after school she was like one of the boys. She could beat every one of us in a game of "Horse" on the basketball court, and could out dribble us, even wearing that cumbersome habit. I figured she must have been a real tomboy growing up, and her younger brothers were probably happy to see her go into the convent.

She also taught me a valuable life lesson during the baseball season. Holy Trinity would play against other local schools that season, and the team elected me captain. But because I wasn't any good at catching the ball, I didn't even make the first team. Complaining to Sister Rose Thomas while sitting on the bench, she explained to me that this was actually a good thing as this showed leadership that would help me in the future. I did buy into that logic – but decided to play lacrosse when I got to high school.

Thanks to Rose Thomas I did quite well academically that year, and with my final grades and a recommendation from her, I was accepted at nearby Deerfield Academy, a well-regarded boarding school that selected a small number of local boys each year to attend as day students.

Thanks to the foundation provided by Holy Trinity, and especially my grammar school "Book Ends," Sisters Agnes Angela and Rose Thomas, I was able to handle the more demanding academic schedule Deerfield offered. The Academy provided excellent masters including my sophomore English teacher, Mr. Binswanger, who is the only person to ever give me a grade below zero. It was on my initial essay that year – he actually gave me a minus sixty, a clear indication of how far I needed to progress during the fall semester. And then there was Bryce Lambert, a true man of letters, who introduced us to Steinbeck, Hemingway, and A. J. Cronin among others, instilling a life-long interest in the joy of reading a good book.

Deerfield led to Georgetown and a team of Jesuits who force-fed us Theology, Logic and Philosophy, along with an impressive team of professors, especially in my major of history and political science. The result of those four wonderful years was a somewhat belated, but all important "Now I get it!" moment when one finally grasps how each of the disciplines previously studied interrelate. Along with music and art, this ever evolving circle of knowledge represented not the end, but only the beginning of a lifetime of learning. As I reflect on all the men and women who contributed to my years of formal education, I inevitably come back to those early years and my two favorite Sisters of St. Joseph, my "Book Ends."

While at Georgetown I learned that two of my own sisters decided to join the Sisters of St. Joseph, and the next time I saw them they were wearing the same habits I was introduced to on that first day of school. They went on to teach in various schools in western Massachusetts, and frequently when we got together, they would mention that they had recently seen Sister Agnes Angela or Sister Rose Thomas, and the older sisters always asked how

I was doing. Sister Agnes Angela died a good number of years ago, but just last fall my sister, Maureen, called to tell me that Rose Thomas had passed away at the community nursing home. She added that even on her last visit Rose Thomas asked about me and my family.

In the early 70s, the Sisters of St. Joseph elected to modify the original habits, and a few years later moved to contemporary women's clothing with only a simple cross identifying their calling. At the same time they reverted to their given and family names. I was happy about these changes for my own sisters; nevertheless whenever my "Book Ends" came up in a discussion, I was never interested in seeing a current photograph of them in normal dress, nor in learning that their real names were Kathy Sheehan or Patty Grogan, or something like that. For me, my "Book Ends" would always be in their proper "God's Dress" while being addressed by their religious names.

While they continue to enjoy that special place in heaven set aside for those women who chose a religious life on earth, I hope they realize there are students who still remember them fondly.

Thank you, ladies, for a job well done!

God's Dress

FENWAY

IN THE BEGINNING, FENWAY, home to the Boston Red Sox, was, in my mind, a magical place, created from the sounds I heard as I faithfully listened to the Sox games on our family radio. This mental image was occasionally enhanced by black and white game photos displayed in the Sports section of our local newspaper. It became an important part of my life from an early age as it did for so many of my friends living in western Massachusetts where the Red Sox were a passion. With my book of scorecards on my lap, I listened to every game I possibly could from the time I was in first grade. Well, not every game, as some evenings the Red Sox were pre-empted in the Broughan household by those all important radio shows such as "Jack Benny Show" or "The Great Gildersleeves" as my parents and sisters sat around the radio for their evening entertainment. As soon as those "hateful" shows were over, it was back to Fenway and the melodious voice of Russ Hodges providing his eloquent play-by-play description of the antics of my favorite sports heroes.

During those early years, as huge a fan as I was, my only entry into Fenway was through my imagination while listening to games on the radio. An actual visit was not likely because of the distance to Boston - ninety-nine miles as the crow flies, I was told - not to mention the cost of getting to the park, and buying those expensive $5.00 grandstand tickets. So, I cannot tell you how excited I was to learn that the Red Sox organization was hosting the Holy Trinity altar boys to a night game the summer after I completed fourth grade.

As the bus headed for Boston that afternoon, it seemed like those ninety-nine miles would never end. Finally, we were there. And even before we entered the ball park the atmosphere around Fenway was even more exciting than anything I had conjured up in my mind. Fellow Red

Sox fans of all ages and all sizes, most with Red Sox hats and shirts, moved toward the turnstiles, while hawkers sold peanuts in the bag, or called out, "Programs . . . Programs only a dime" on their small boxes near the entrance. It was unreal – almost like being in a movie.

When it was time to enter Fenway, we moved forward with the crowd through the gates into the cavernous, dark concrete hall and headed up the narrow ramp to our seats in far right field. In spite of the years spent envisioning what Fenway looked like, nothing could have prepared me for my first glimpse of the field as I walked into the stands and saw it for the first time. The grass was so green… greener and more perfect than any grass I have ever seen before and made even brighter by the giant lights that surrounded the entire ball park, serving as large beacons to the thousands of summer flies that joined the party. And there it was – the Green Monster, bigger and higher than I even expected. How could Ted Williams have hit so many home runs over that wall and onto the same street I had just left!

And there they were – Johnny Pesky, Ted Lepcio and Dom DiMaggio (the Yankees had Joe, but we Sox fans knew his brother Dom was better) with their blindingly white uniforms with the red lettering spelling out "Red Sox." In that instant I experienced an immediate mental photo that was indelibly imprinted on my brain as a life-long memory I carry with me to this day.

I devoured every minute of that special night, as well as devouring the peanuts I bought outside and ate like I have never had one before. I also enjoyed the incredibly delicious, though soggy, hot dog with Gulden's mustard. My Mother always bought French's, but this night I realized that Gulden's was much better. And I continue to use it, with relish, to this day. To make the night even more special, it was "Bobby Doerr Night," honoring the best second baseman in the club's history. They even gave him a new car, which he drove around the field to the ecstatic cheers from the fans.

And so, the initial fear that Fenway in reality might not be the magical place my mind had created over the years was quickly and completely dispelled. I really felt nothing could ever top that night at Fenway. Little did I know on that evening another visit to the greatest ball park in America six years later would accomplish that – in spades!

In 1957, the summer after my sophomore year at Deerfield, I remained a loyal Red Sox fan, so I decided to enter the annual contest to select the "Red Sox Junior Broadcaster of the Year." The contest started with my submitting an essay indicating the reasons why I deserved to be considered. Whatever I wrote was apparently sufficient to receive an actual response from the team directing me to my local radio station that broadcast the games in our area. There I was interviewed by our local sports announcer who forwarded the tape to Boston. To my great surprise and delight I received a congratulatory telegram in early August inviting my parents and me to dinner at the Kenmore Square Hotel prior to a night game against the Washington Senators. It was signed by Curt Gowdy, then the popular voice of the Boston Red Sox.

Now a teenager, and much more mature and cool than that young impressionable altar boy, I took the news in stride. Nevertheless, I must admit I really was quite excited about my return to Fenway, and once we arrived in Boston that afternoon, I realized what a thrill it was to be having dinner with Curt Gowdy and his side-kick, Bob Allen.

Following that early dinner, we walked across the street to Fenway, and on this visit, instead of climbing up to the right field grandstand, I was actually brought down to the field itself and to the Red Sox dugout. Yes, on to the actual ball field! And there I was, shaking hands with Jackie Jensen, Sammy White and even the mercurial Jimmy Piersall. As exciting as this was, there was more. Curt then led me up to the broadcasting booth and gave me a chair between himself and Bob Allen as they prepared to broadcast the game. What a view, looking out onto the lighted field, and there I was in the very booth that these same two announcers used to broadcast every game I had listened to for years. Could this night get any better? It was during the fourth inning that I was told that I would be providing the play-by-play announcing for the eighth inning live throughout New England! Curt said he did not want to tell me earlier, as he did not want to make me overly nervous. Overly nervous?? I began to think of all the buzz words and lingo used by Gowdy, Mel Allen and the other great announcers I had listened to over the years as I mentally prepared for my big moment.

The top of the eighth inning arrived, the red light in the booth goes on and the Senators' first baseman, Roy Sievers, clicks his cleats, rubs his hands and steps into the batter's box. The Sox starter, Billy Mombouquette, looks in and delivers a fast ball to Sievers for strike one. I delivered the information to the thousands of listening fans without a flaw in my extremely excited, high-pitched voice. No, I wasn't nervous! Sievers then lines the next pitch to left, and again, flawlessly I thought, I announced that Sievers hits a line-drive single to left. Except the ball was hit directly to Ted Williams (my all-time baseball hero), who takes a few steps toward the infield and catches the ball belt high. What now? I immediately correct myself saying, "Williams makes a great fielding play to rob Sievers of a base hit!" Thank goodness it was radio, which allows a very nervous junior announcer the license to improvise – something that was lost with the arrival of television on the sports scene. The remainder of the first half of the eighth inning was uneventful, much to my relief.

In the bottom of the eighth, the second batter for the Sox was the great man himself, Ted Williams, and does he not hit a line drive home run into the center field bleachers. All of New England heard my description of that "historic Narragansett Blast" as my voice grew louder and higher in my excitement of witnessing and having the privilege of announcing to the world yet another Ted Williams home run.

Following the game, it was decided by an amused Gowdy and Allen that Ted, himself, should hear about his excellent defensive play in the eighth inning. Ted was not known as a great defensive player, but who cared given his hitting prowess. Thus a tongue-tied junior broadcaster was brought to the dressing room along with my father to meet, in person, the baseball legend himself. Ted was most gracious, but, honestly, to this day, being so nervous, I do not remember any part of the historic (at least in my mind) conversation that took place.

However, as we left Fenway that night, still in somewhat of a daze, I realized that Fenway had, yet again, given me a memory I would never forget.

A few years later, I went off to college and then to Chicago to work, marry, have children and attend the Chicago Cubs and Bears games, so that my first love, the Boston Red Sox, took a back seat in my life. Thirty years later, however, I happened to be in Boston for a trade show during a summer weekend. The Sox were on the road that weekend. Nevertheless, on a free evening, I felt myself drawn back to Fenway, even though there was no game. Walking from my Back Bay hotel I arrived at the ballpark just as the sun was setting. Unlike a home game night, it was quiet and still on that very warm evening. A few bars around Fenway were open and I could hear sports talk from the patrons while they drank beer and watched the Sox away game on TV. I walked around the entire park, knowing that I had it to myself. I swear I could even smell the stale beer and Gulden's mustard that over the many years had become an integral part of the ancient cement floors just inside the locked gates.

As I reminisced, I realized what an important role Fenway played in my earlier life, and those incredible memories it has provided me. Even without the bustling crowds, the color, the lights and sounds of baseball, I could not have had a better evening, reliving the past and enjoying the moment.

Curt Gowdy and Friends in Broadcast Booth

A Lifetime of Friendships

"SORRY, I DON'T HAVE a clue," I answered my mother as I held up two long cloth strips discovered in a gift box she presented to me at our family Labor Day picnic. I was off the next morning to start my college career at Georgetown University, and this was my going away party. My mother finally explained the mysterious important gift was her apron strings. Tomorrow a new phase of my life was to begin, and I was now officially "on my own." And what a perfect place to start this new phase – Georgetown University in the heart of our nation's capital. Recognizing the financial sacrifices my parents would be making, I was determined to make the most out of the next four years, and that is exactly what I did.

Georgetown was a perfect fit for me. I loved the location, the Jesuit orientated curriculum, and the many activities in the Washington, DC area available to students. And I was far enough away from home to be truly on my own, yet close enough to return during school holidays and summer vacation. (Although difficult to believe in this day and age, my most frequent mode of transportation between DC and New England was hitch hiking with my good friend and traveling companion, John Dolan, who lived in nearby Brighton, Massachusetts.) Without a doubt, the most important decision I made that first semester, was to try out for the Georgetown Chimes, the popular a capella singing group on campus. I must admit that my freshman year as a neophyte trying to earn membership in the group was sometimes challenging and not always pleasant. But, even then, I realized that my association with the Chimes would offer many special experiences during the next three years. Little did I realize that following graduation my fellow Chimes would remain lifelong friends, and even today, I cherish those special occasions when we get together and attempt to still create "awe inspiring" harmony.

While the group was founded in 1946, and I became an alumnus in late spring of 1964, the Chimes continue to be a major presence at Georgetown today. An important Chimes tradition which began in my senior year when I was Ephus (head honcho) continues to be a special feature of the group's legacy. The events that bonded our 1964 group together that spring continue today, and I would be remiss if I did not tell the tales of my last semester with the Chimes.

The initial concept of a relationship with the newly opened 1789 Restaurant and the Chimes was established in early January, 1964, between its founder, Richard McCooey, and myself during a meeting set up by our mutual friend, Frank Gannon. Frank was President of the Yard that year, worked at the '89 and was a good friend of our group (and subject of my next chapter). McCooey had expressed to Frank an interest in developing a relationship with the Chimes similar to the long-standing weekly concert the Wiffenpoofs performed at Morey's near the Yale campus.

To replicate that tradition, it was agreed that the Chimes would sing each Friday afternoon in the Pub portion of the '89 restaurant. Signs were made and posted around campus inviting students and faculty to join us. From late February to mid-March, these weekly sets attracted little interest and a small audience, primarily friends who were offered a free beer to show up.

By mid-March, we agreed that this initial concept was not working – perhaps the wrong time of day, wrong location – and definitely too genteel for our group; it was not the Chimes' style. So, it was agreed that we would change the timing and location to a Wednesday night set in the Tombs, the popular student rathskellar in the basement of the restaurant. Richard felt a large table in front of the fireplace would work and had his technicians rig a few speakers with a feed into the Tombs sound system, mixed with a set of overhead lights. Quite elementary, but it worked. So another set of posters announcing the new venue was displayed around the campus in hopes students in addition to our small group of "Chime Buffs," still looking for the same free beer, would show up.

The weeks leading up to that first Chimes Night were quite busy and successful for us – including a sold-out concert in Gaston Hall. So, as we headed to the Tombs that Wednesday night, we were feeling pretty good about ourselves, but clearly unsure how this new concept would work. To our pleasant surprise, we arrived to find an overflowing boisterous crowd awaiting us, with an even larger group waiting patiently up the stairs and down the street. Initially, we thought this huge showing was due to our popularity on campus, but then we quickly realized that Thursday was a Holy Day and there were no classes, so students were out to party.

Once seated at the table, mugs and bottles of Black Horse Ale were generously supplied to our group by the staff. Then, the room went dark, the crowd hushed and the lights came on over the table. Before we completed "We Meet," we looked at each other and knew we were embarking on something special. The set ended to great cheers, and the appreciative crowd was ready for more. So that initial set lead to additional ones well into the night. It was a true party, and we were enjoying every minute of it – right up to "last call" (and beyond)! McCooey also enjoyed the night, calling it magical, and we immediately agreed that Chimes Night at the Tombs would continue every Wednesday night until the late May end of the semester. (GU cost much less then, and the school year was longer.)

The word of that first Chimes Night spread quickly and every Wednesday night for the remainder of the spring brought out enthusiastic crowds. Even the *Washington Post* reported in the entertainment section that Wednesday nights in the Tombs was "the new hot spot," bringing students from surrounding schools as well.

Before the last event in May, both McCooey and ourselves realized a special bond between the Chimes and the '89 had been established which, hopefully, would continue in the future. So confident was McCooey that he ordered the brass plate for "The Chimes Table," as well as the double handed Chime mugs from a pewter company in the UK.

On many evenings, McCooey would host our group upstairs for upstairs for quiet songs and long conversations on many subjects that should be part of every college education – especially when appropriate amounts of alcohol were included. Sometimes a special party was planned, such as our own "Tom Jones" dinner, reenacting one of the greatest scenes in the history of film. On graduation night, McCooey even provided a late night evening for our parents, which Mom and Dad declared was the highlight of graduation weekend.

Because our Chime group was, and is, so important to me, I need to include each of them in this memoir chapter, starting with John O'Brien (With whom I shared a summer travel expedition around the country after graduation. Our plan was to replicate John Steinbeck's *Travels with Charlie,"* except our "Charlie" was not a dog, but a Styrofoam cooler filled with ice cold Coors from the streams of Colorado), Phil Murray, Mike Fackler, (Dr.) Fred Cosco, Perry Butler, Neil Scanell, Tim Mattimore and three true "One of a Kind" personalities – Kevin O'Brien, Don Colleton and (Dr.) Bill Edgerton.

Our good friend, Richard McCooey, passed away last year. While he was never a Chime, we always felt he was part of us. After singing at his funeral at Holy Trinity Church in Georgetown last September, our group awaited him outside the church. Before his casket was returned to the hearse, a special Chimes blue and white striped tie was laid over the casket, a proper farewell to a great friend whose memory lives on in each of us and also through the young active Chimes who gather around that special table in the Tombs each week.

Georgetown Chimes - 1964

FRANK

Note: The catalyst for starting my memoir was Jack Galvin's course for Circle of Scholars at Salve Regina University. Each week Jack would select a topic for an essay we then shared the following week with our fellow writers. One topic was, "A fascinating or memorable person in your life." Even though it had been some forty years since last visiting with him, Frank's name immediately came to mind.

THERE WAS NO REASON that Frank and I should become friends. Our relationship began on a somewhat adversarial note during junior year at Georgetown University. As chairman of the Junior Prom Committee representing the College, I was responsible for recommending a headliner for the concert to be held on the eve of the dance. My choice was the Peter Duchin Band, immensely popular on the college circuit that year. Frank was my counterpart representing the School of Foreign Service at Georgetown. His choice was a "relatively unknown" blues singer by the name of Ray Charles. Much to my amazement and disappointment, the Joint Prom Committee sided with Frank, and I reluctantly accepted defeat, confident that Ray Charles would be a "bust." A few days later, Frank sought me out on campus and offered me two tickets to join him at the concert, a most conciliatory gesture on his part, I thought. Ray Charles was sensational, with the sold-out crowd on its feet throughout the event, and the initial animosity between us quickly turned into mutual respect.

Nevertheless, a real friendship with Frank remained improbable, as our personalities and life styles could not have been more dissimilar. Frank was incredibly smart, a true cum laude scholar, while my grade average – well, I'd rather not talk about it. And while my reading list was popular fiction, he was reading biography or history. My relaxation featured a sporting event or "beer talking" at Max's Pub, while Frank was enjoying a concert or a Broadway musical. (I later discovered he knew every word of every song of every Broadway musical of the past ten years – including the forgettable *110 Degrees in the Shade.*) In fact, our personalities could not have been more different. I tended to be very gregarious, and as uncomplicated as an open book. Frank was more introspective, almost reticent, with a quite distinct manner of speaking that was annoyingly intriguing. Being rather short and somewhat scholarly in appearance – sometimes he even actually wore a bow tie – he could have easily been mistaken for an absent-minded professor. Yet, the glint in his eyes and his wry humor let you know that he was one step ahead of you and knew exactly what he wanted in life.

During the remainder of the spring semester we did not see much of each other, but did enjoy our brief encounters. Frank played piano four nights a week at the trendy 1789 Restaurant, near campus, which was a Mecca for Washington's political elite. He once told me that he played to help pay his way through Georgetown, although the real intent was to meet the "movers and shakers" that were part of the Kennedy administration. Soon Frank was entertaining at parties for Washington's select few – including dinner parties hosted by Kennedy himself on the presidential yacht *Sequoia*.

Meanwhile, I was a part of a popular, fun-loving Georgetown singing group, called the Chimes. So while Frank was hobnobbing with Washington's rich and famous, the Chimes were singing in any local bar to earn a free round of beer, or at a local college to meet the girls. To my amazement, Frank, when he had an opportunity to join us, preferred being with our rowdy crowd where it tended to be boisterous and spontaneous – something quite different from being part of the Washington elite crowd. Frank even found a way to bring these two disparate groups together. Thanks to his introductions, the Chimes were suddenly invited to sing at some of the major events around town – even providing entertainment for parties hosted by the Attorney General, Robert Kennedy, both in his office and at his Virginia home. It was great times for all, and Frank became an honorary member of our group.

In our senior year Frank became President of the Yard, Georgetown University's top student officer. This, and his continued insistence on studying, limited the amount of time we all got together. When he found time to join us, he seemed to really enjoy those beer-driven antics that were so different from his structured, scholarly lifestyle. Toward the end of our senior year, we included Frank in one of our most outrageous activities yet on a spring night at the Washington Marina near National Airport. After a few too many beers on that warm evening, we decided that the rental sailboats might as well be used to cross the nearby cove to the airport runway. Once there we decided to lie down on our backs with arms and legs extended, taking inspiration from Leonardo Da Vinci's *Vitruvian Man.* From this ridiculous position we could then watch the late night planes fly directly above our heads to land 150 yards behind us. It was a miracle that we were not injured, or at the very least arrested. When we returned to the campus, I felt somewhat guilty about the fact that we had finally corrupted this reserved, cautious scholar and student leader by putting him through that somewhat crazy "last hurrah" prior to graduation. That guilt dissipated when Frank turned to me and exclaimed that the evening's caper was one of the most fun late nights he had during his four years at Georgetown.

Following our late May graduation, we decided to remain in D.C. for the month of June and work together as bartenders at the 1789, sharing a small, hot room above a launderette next to the restaurant. Working long hours, we would often, after closing the bar around 2 am, enjoy breakfast or a few beers while talking about life and our future plans as the sun came up.

The long evenings spent bartending left little time for socializing. Leave it to Frank to somehow garner two invitations to the most sought after event of the social season – a debutante garden party for the great great granddaughter of the 19th century railroad magnate, Jay Gould, at the family estate located in the exclusive horse country of nearby Maryland. The invitation was not without cost, though, as we both had to rent tuxedos for the occasion. Worse, an expensive auto also had to be rented, as one could not possibly arrive in a Chevy or a Ford.

The party for some two hundred guests was set in a spacious, beautifully decorated garden (where there were enough strings of white lights to decorate a thousand Christmas trees) overlooking a pasture of horses enjoying the last rays of a setting sun. You could not have been more impressed with the "over-the-top" conspicuous consumption both in the massive house and on the lawn. There had to be a minimum of fifty waiters in white tie and tails, all relentless in their constant serving of the finest Moet & Chandon Champagne as well as elegant hors d'oeuvres. In addition, there were large tables overflowing with magnificent food. There were even barrels of ice located around the garden filled with bottles of champagne so one could serve himself if so desired.

Quite dapper in our rental outfits, and on our best behavior, we enjoyed the evening immensely – especially knowing that our middle class butts should not even have been there in the first place. Finally, late into the evening, the ample amount of champagne that we consumed finally won out. Appropriately inebriated, we decided to take advantage or the self service barrels and loaded up with properly chilled bottles of that excellent Moet under our jackets – and made off to our waiting rental car, cruising back to reality. As we popped open two bottles to enjoy on our trip to our Georgetown apartment, the drive home gave new meaning to "one for the road." Although suffering a life-threatening hangover the next morning, we both agreed the evening was a fitting closure to our last month at Georgetown before going off to face the real world.

A week later we both moved on. Frank was headed to London for three years as a Fulbright Scholar studying at the London School of Economics, while I went on a mindless, but most enjoyable, driving tour of the U.S. with another college friend. As Frank and I departed D.C., we vowed to keep in touch. During the subsequent 48 years, we have gotten together on only a few occasions. Nevertheless, as I had come to expect, these meetings were both eventful and enjoyable. And, they even included a glimpse into the lives of two modern Shakespearian characters – one a victorious leader, Winston Churchill, and the other a tragic "king," Richard M. Nixon.

Our first reunion was two years later. I was living in New York and working for Pan Am when I was scheduled for a week of training in London. I called Frank, hoping we could spend the weekend together before my classes began. He was excited about the visit and planned to meet me at the airport when I arrived. I expected a leisurely visit with some sightseeing and a few pints in the London pubs. I should have remembered that with Frank, you should expect the unexpected.

He met me at outside of Customs, and led me to the nearby train station, advising that we had been invited to Randolph Churchill's country home, Stour House in Suffolk, for a special luncheon. On the train, he brought me up-to-date on his life in London. While at the London School of Economics he had been hired by Randolph Churchill to assist in researching and writing Randolph's planned seven volume definitive biography of his father, Winston.

Upon arrival, I was introduced to the gathered guests including his son, Winston (soon to be a Member of Parliament), as well as the editor of the London *Times* and the garden editor of the *Telegraph* (her title explaining the dirt under her fingernails). Two younger gentlemen were immediately recognizable. The first was an American, Tom Leher, the popular satirist from Harvard, and a favorite of Randolph's. The second was David Frost, well known to Americans for his weekly TV show *That Was The Week That Was*. At first glance, I must admit that David Frost was much more impressive on TV than he was in person. The highlight of the luncheon party was the planned consumption of the last bottles of Winston's favorite champagne from the extensive wine cellar. Listening to our host, it appeared he started his tasting of the bubbly earlier in the day. As I took in the eclectic group of guests, with as many dogs as humans in attendance, it felt surreal, like I was in a modern version of a Hogarth painting. The gentlemen retired to the library for port and cigars while Randolph pontificated on the "glories of the nation." The discussion of the "glories" led to Dame Margot Fonteyn, and I was forced to admit that I had never heard of the greatest ballerina of the time. Randolph immediately called Covent Garden to confirm that the VIP box overlooking stage left was available for the evening, and then sent Frank and me off to London to see the sold out performance of *Swan Lake* featuring Margot Fonteyn and her equally famous young partner, Rudolph Nureyev. It was an amazing evening culminating in a 10-minute standing ovation and a stage strewn with roses.

My unbelievable introduction to London ended by sharing Frank's tiny five hundred year old dorm room at the university. After the overnight flight and the remarkable day, I slept twelve hours on the floor and awoke to an amazing room, making me think I was in a modern day Dickens's novel. As we parted after lunch Frank promised he would contact me as soon as he returned to the States.

Frank did not return that summer, as planned. Instead he traveled to Viet Nam where he spent the next two years as a reporter on the war. As the years went by, I heard that he had returned to Washington and had joined the Nixon White House as a speech writer. The next time we made contact was in spring of 1974. I was married to my wife, Winnie, and Frank came for dinner in our Chicago apartment. Most recently he had resigned his White House position to take a job working for Jack Valenti, President of the Motion Picture Association of America. He was trading the drama of Washington politics for the excitement of Hollywood. On his final day at the White House he was called to the President's office for the official handshake and commemorative picture. Instead, Frank went on to regale us with the scene that met him that day. There was the sitting President, in despair, pleading with Frank not to leave him in his hour of need. After much conversation, Frank capitulated and agreed to stay on, even though his furniture, now on the way to LA, was "somewhere around Sandusky, OH." In a true to life impersonation, Frank told us of Nixon, missing the point entirely, going off on a tangent about what a wonderful place Sandusky was – at least as seen from the platform of his campaign train! As it turned out, Frank and his White House speech writing partner, Diane Sawyer, stayed with Nixon to the bitter end, and accompanied the President and his family on the lonely Air Force One flight to San Clemente. Frank remained with Nixon and in 1977 was instrumental in arranging a series of interviews between his boss and the same David Frost I dined with in England. These interviews are now considered an important part of the Nixon legacy.

Years go by and the Broughan clan moved to Alexandria, Virginia as I took a position in Washington, D.C. I had heard that Frank and Diane had also returned to the area – Frank working for one of the "think tanks," and Diane was a correspondent for CBS News. Frank and I met for lunch and decided that a longer Saturday night dinner at our home was in order. Since we had recently moved with three children four and under, Winnie was not particularly thrilled about entertaining the glamorous CBS reporter. I had run into Frank and Diane (who was without makeup and wearing glasses) at a DC store the week before and I assured my wife that Diane was actually quite plain, so she had nothing to fear. The night of the dinner, the doorbell rings and we greet Frank and the very glamorous, well-dressed Diane. I felt a swift kick connect with my ankle – was it my fault I misjudged how great Diane actually looked? As it turned out, she was a delightful guest – our small children named a fish in the family aquarium Diane the next morning, and she won points when (after a phone call to let CBS know where they could reach her) she told Winnie how she envied her home and family life.

A dozen years later I found Frank to invite him to a special lunch at our home in conjunction with the Chimes 50th Anniversary Concert at Georgetown. At the time Frank was a writer and co-producer for the *Late Night with David Letterman Show,* and planned to take a shuttle to National Airport for our Saturday afternoon lunch. On the day of the concert, lunch was served but there was no Frank. Just as I was about to leave to go to rehearsals for the concert, a taxi pulled up in front of the house, and "better late than never" Frank appears. He accompanied me to the rehearsal to say hello to his old Chime friends, most of whom hadn't seen him since graduation, nearly 30 years ago. As I drove him back to the airport, he talked about how much he enjoyed the brief visit with old friends, and how it brought back great memories. He said he would definitely stay in touch and would make the effort to attend one of our annual Chime reunions. The years flew by with our next encounter an all too brief visit during our 50th Reunion at Georgetown.

My most recent "Frank sighting" was on a flight from Paris to Boston a few years ago where they showed the *Nixon Frost* film. Frank is a character in the movie, an assistant and coach to Nixon during the interviews. It was a small part, but I was struck by what an unattractive, geeky looking actor Ron Howard had chosen to play Frank. While he was no Brad Pitt, as a friend I believed he deserved better.

I wonder, as the years continue to go by, if we will have the opportunity to get together again. I do hope so but I tend to doubt it given his busy schedule, including his work at the Nixon Library in California. If it should happen, I am sure it will be, as always, a most stimulating and enjoyable experience. Frank will always be a fascinating mystery to me. And, as a friend, he has enriched my life.

Frank and friends enjoying a *Tom Jones* dinner at the *1789*.

A Memory from One
of the "Dwindling Few"

The inauguration of John F. Kennedy as the 35th President of the
United States, Friday, January 20, 1961

L AST YEAR AFTER WORKING my way through the first 178 pages of ads, I came upon a special *Vanity Fair* feature detailing the glamorous and memorable inauguration of John F. Kennedy – complete with photos of the new president with the celebrities and movie stars that made it such a gala event.

I was immediately struck and disturbed by the opening paragraph that read something like this, "For the dwindling few still alive who attended that once-in-a-lifetime event." Good God, they are talking about me! No matter that I was only nineteen at the time; I am part of those "dwindling few." Clearly it was time to record the memories of my own participation that incredible day when JFK boldly proclaimed, "Ask not what your country can do for you…"

Long before I arrived in Washington in early September, 1960, I had been an ardent supporter of JFK. After all, I was living in western Massachusetts and Kennedy was my senator. And, as my mother kept reminding me, he was an Irish Catholic Democrat. However, supporting JFK for president was a lonely endeavor for me while attending Deerfield Academy. Almost all of my classmates were sons of traditional conservative Republicans. They assured me that America was definitely not ready to elect a Catholic as our president. Plus JFK had graduated from Choate, an arch enemy of Deerfield. I was undeterred, however, in my support and admiration, especially after devouring my newly acquired first edition of his incredible *Profiles in Courage* in one sitting. Having never heard of a ghost writer, I was quite impressed he had the time to write such a great book himself, while also working tirelessly as my senator - when not sailing on the Cape.

It was early during my senior year at Deerfield that my father attended a newspaper publishers meeting in Boston where JFK gave the keynote address. I gave him my copy of *Profiles* with instructions not to return home until JFK had personally autographed the book. You cannot believe my delight when he returned the book to me and there on the first page it read, "To John. With very warmest regards, John Kennedy."

The next spring, Kennedy was well on his way toward winning the Democratic nomination later that summer. One evening, bored with my homework assignments, I picked up my precious possession and carefully analyzed the Kennedy signature. I noticed that it was somewhat careless in style with an incomplete letter J in his first name. His K needed help as well. So with my own ballpoint pen, I fixed it.

I arrived at Georgetown to start my freshman year that September when the presidential campaign was in full swing. Two months later I was elated when my candidate was elected our 35th President.

The Georgetown neighborhood was particularly exciting immediately after the election as the president-elect and Jackie were living a few blocks from the university in their townhouse on N Street. In fact, one afternoon some friends and I stopped Kennedy to congratulate him on his victory as he and Jackie were taking a stroll along Wisconsin Avenue. In January, with the inauguration only a few weeks away, I would often walk down to the Kennedy home where JFK would introduce his newest cabinet nominees from his front stoop. It is hard to believe in this day and age of security and excessive media coverage that there would only be a dozen or so members of the press and a handful of spectators watching these rather low-key announcements.

While quite excited about the upcoming inaugural, I expected to be watching it on a TV in our dorm or at a local bar on nearby M Street. Little could I have imagined that Mother Nature would provide me a front row seat for one of the most memorable days in our country's history.

The only event I did expect to experience firsthand was an inaugural concert the evening before the big day. I was a member of the Georgetown Glee Club, featured at the concert in historic Constitution Hall. As we arrived at the auditorium in our tuxes that evening, we walked through more than eight inches of fresh snow, and it was still snowing. The concert itself was a great success, and it was a special treat for all of us on that stage to look out toward the balcony where JFK and Jackie glowed radiantly enjoying the adulation of a glittering audience below them. With the concert over and the snow still falling, we were told the Army was now shoveling the length of Pennsylvania Avenue in preparation for the parade the next afternoon.

"Why don't we head toward that area for a warm and cozy bar on K Street to watch the action," I proposed to a few friends. Later, trudging through more than a foot of snow back to campus in the wee hours of the morning, well fortified for the blizzard conditions, we decided to return to the Capitol the next day to see if we might watch the Inauguration in person. After all, the airports had been shut down and thousands of guests planning to attend simply would not make it into DC for the planned events.

One of the most unforgettable days of my young life began after only a few hours of sleep. As my memory has aged as effectively as the rest of my body, the most accurate version of this special day can be found in a letter I excitedly wrote to my parents. The letter was shared
Around The Clock

by my father with the staff at the Greenfield *Recorder*, and a feature writer on the staff found it to be of sufficient interest to use it as the basis of an article in the February 1, 1961 edition.

Music Gets Greenfield Boy "Inside" Washington

By WAYNE A. SMITH
February 1, 1996--A little bit of music can do a lot for a guy. The guy in our story is a handsome young Greenfield tenor and how he got to meet the 35th President of the U.S.A.

Jack Broughan, son of Mr. and Mrs. John Broughan of 31 Garfield Street, and a first-year student at Georgetown University, is still in a daze with excitement. As a member of the University Glee Club and "Chimes," a select vocal group of 11, he won ringside glimpses of many of the most colorful aspects of the inauguration. Jack grew up in Greenfield, attended Holy Trinity School, and then went to Deerfield Academy from which he was graduated last June. While at Deerfield his fine tenor voice won the attention of Ralph Oatley, director of music, who put him in the glee club. He also had a featured role in last year's operetta, "The Red Mill." He was in the glee club three years.

At Georgetown he has been enjoying advantages to be gained through concert appearances in the Washington area and elsewhere. He will be singing in New York and St. Louis, Mo., next month with the group.

The Georgetown University Glee Club participated in the inaugural concert in Constitution Hall. And like all others engaged in the festivities there were many problems to be surmounted because of the snowstorm.

JACK'S LETTER this past week to his family describes some of the adversities along with the thrilling experience he had along the sidelines. It follows in part:

"Well, it's all over and I still can't believe it. On Thursday night we were walking down in Georgetown where there was a party given by Kennedy's sister, Mrs. S. Smith. We stood around and watched Kennedy come out, along with Sinatra, Tony Curtis, Janet Leigh, Milton Berle and the governors. Sinatra came out on the porch and sang for us.

"Thursday was the start of the big weekend. I just read that tickets were non-existent. It may have been right if it hadn't snowed all day Thursday and screwed everything up. By 6 o'clock everything had stopped. Our bus had to drive on the wrong side of the street to get us to Constitution Hall. Traveling was such a problem to the hall, which had been completely sold out, that it was half empty. Howard University didn't get there so we (Georgetown) had to sing the whole 'declaration' by ourselves.

"Kennedy and Jackie along with the Johnsons were there. Jackie looked like a Greek goddess sitting there in her white satin gown listening to us sing. What a great couple. I hope you heard us (and Tony Marvin) and enjoyed us. If you did, you know that Kennedy left right after we sang.

"We were told we could get in free to the Gala, but there was no way of getting over there. Now I wished I had walked those 25 blocks. You just could not believe how messed up the city was that night. It took an hour for a car to move a block.

* * *

"AFTER ONLY about three hours' sleep we got up and went to 9 o'clock Mass at Holy Trinity. You will never guess who sat two rows in front of us. Yep! Jack was there. Just think: we were at the first inauguration Mass in history.

"Then we left for the Capital with hopes of catching a glimpse of the inauguration itself. Being college students, we could not be stopped. We snuck into the box seats and sat in about the 12th row, 25 feet from the platform and had the most perfect view of the whole show. It was the most thrilling spectacle I have ever seen. On TV you could probably have seen the back of my head.

"Robert Frost was great and Kennedy's speech was the greatest I have ever heard. I was really moved by the whole thing. We watched the parade, first from across the art museum, and later moved up and snuck into the $25 seats across from Kennedy's reviewing stand.

"We got back to school about 7 'o'clock exhausted, cold and extremely happy, in a daze (I still am). Dave Scannell came in and told me to put on my tuxedo, we were singing at a pre-inauguration dinner party. A car came to pick us up; believe it or not, it was one of those long black boats with the flags in the front like Kennedy had been driving in all day. So we were driven to the party – guess who ___Steve Smith, Kennedy's brother-in-law.

"We went to the Shoreham with

the Chimes. At one point we were in a room singing when in came Hollins and his wife, Pat, the governor of South Carolina, who asked us to come and sing for some things down there, which we might do. We met just about every Democrat in Massachusetts. (Didn't see the Sullivans). Kennedy and Johnson came in after midnight and I shook the hands of our President and vice-President of the U.S.; What a thrill.

weekend. Please save this letter as I am still in a daze and might not be able to believe this in a few years. It sure seems impossible. So the "Glee' and 'Chimes' have been great advantages to me this week. It was the greatest week I have ever spent."

The next three years were an amazing time to be in Washington as the Kennedy era brought new life to the city. During that time, the Georgetown Chimes did sing at a few embassy parties where the President was in attendance or made a cameo appearance. In addition, we were also asked by the Attorney General to entertain at a couple of parties given by Bobby Kennedy for his staff and families during the holidays.

But, it came to a shocking end that fateful day in late November during my senior year. I will never forget standing on a street corner near the campus listening to a car radio as Walter Cronkite announced that the president had been shot - or, an hour later, standing in the university quad with a thousand other silent and stunned students, all in denial. We just wanted to leave, to go home to be with our families as we tried to grasp the magnitude of what had just happened that would change our lives forever. And who could ever forget those remarkable days, sitting in disbelief watching the events in the Dallas county jail, the funeral of our fallen president, the flag-covered casket followed by the rider less horse, a small boy saluting his dead father, and the emotional burial in Arlington with the eternal flame and that idyllic view of the nation's Capitol.

"So that was my Inauguration

Following the Christmas break, I returned to Georgetown for my final semester. It was a wonderful six months, but Washington was just not the same without JFK. The Chimes did visit Bobby Kennedy's home that spring to sing at a large BBQ he and Ethel hosted. We also sang "The Yellow Rose of Texas" for President Lyndon Johnson at Harry Truman's 80th birthday party. The city had a different feel. Life moved on, but there was a void; we were simply left with the memory of what had been a special place and time, thanks to the Kennedys.

Two years ago, Winnie and I were visiting a few of her college friends in California. I related the story of my properly correcting JFK's otherwise flawed signature in my *Profiles in Courage.* One of our friends, Frank McAdams, well known for his prodigious memory, remembered seeing a rare books advertisement in a recent *New York Times* book review section, offering a signed first edition of the same publication. A quick check on the Internet and we found it – offered at $28,500!

When I returned to Newport, I picked up my dusty prized possession, once again admiring the fine enhancement I had made to that otherwise authentic JFK signature.

Without those improvements: $28,500!

With my enhancements: Worthless!

For me, as a tangible reminder of a very special time in my life: Priceless!

For this reason, I will always cherish my personal edition of *Profiles,* co-signed by John Kennedy and myself – a reminder that I was fortunate enough to be part of a very special era that will always be known as "Camelot."

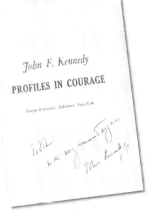

"The Daughter of Time"

"**D**O YOU THINK YOU could teach one course of medieval history as well?" asked Dr. Frank Boyden toward the end of my interview.

"Since my major is history and political science, that should not be a problem," I confidently replied, while carefully omitting that I had never taken a medieval history course, and knew very little about the subject.

It was Thanksgiving break during my senior year at Georgetown. I had decided to continue my studies after graduation with the intention of someday teaching political science at the college level. My plan was to take post graduate courses at the University of Massachusetts at Amherst in the fall, and cover my costs as a dorm master and coach at nearby Deerfield Academy, my alma mater. It was during the meeting to explore such an arrangement that Dr. Boyden suggested the added teaching assignment. I accepted without hesitation.

With this commitment, I rearranged my last semester schedule at Georgetown to audit a course on medieval history, and then planned to spend time during the summer preparing for this teaching assignment.

The summer turned out to be very busy, so a truly neophyte teacher arrived on the Deerfield campus, somewhat ill-prepared and sufficiently nervous about my first job - teaching what I believed at the time a rather boring period of western civilization to young men who were only seven years my junior.

The first weeks went without any major crisis. Lessons were assigned, the major events of the dark ages discussed, and weekly tests given and graded. However, the combination of the subject matter and my obvious inexperience hardly made for an electrifying experience for my sixteen students.

As the fall semester came to a close for Christmas break, I went to my parents' home determined to prepare to wow my class during the winter term. This well-intentioned goal to rise above mediocrity as a teacher hit a road block when I suffered a serious case of pneumonia that resulted in a "delightful" two-week stay in the hospital.

I found myself still recovering as I returned to the classroom in early January to continue where we left off in December. Halfway through that winter term, while my scholars were dreaming about whatever warm destination they would enjoy during spring break, I was contemplating how I could use that time to create real interest and even enthusiasm during the final spring term. At least we would finally be studying the more interesting late medieval period of English kings.

At that moment a bolt of enlightenment hit me!

I remembered a popular historical mystery that made a strong impression on me the previous summer. Josephine Tey's *The Daughter of Time* described a modern day Scotland Yard inspector who had been injured on duty and was hospitalized. While recovering, he was given a book, which led him to believe that Richard III did not kill his nephews, the young princes, in the Tower of London. Inspector Grant asked friends to bring him other books and documents on the subject, which resulted in a significantly different impression of the English king. In fact, the more he studied, the more he became convinced that Richard was a strong, valiant leader who had been framed by the writers who perpetuated the myth. Intrigued by this thesis, I did my own research and discovered a large and committed group of historians who felt so strongly about the revisionist history that they set up an association to prove the errors of the popular Shakespearian image of this disgraced monarch. As the winter term came none too quickly to an end, I formulated a plan for the upcoming spring term, there would be a definite change in the course of the course.

While my "sixteen" headed home in mid-March, I headed to New York City to study more of the Richard III controversy and to purchase sixteen copies of *The Daughter of Time*. Two weeks later when classes resumed, I was determined to no longer be a mediocre teacher, but would join the ranks of Bryce Lambert, Bob McGlynn, and others who had challenged and excited me when a student in these same classrooms not so many years ago.

It was a beautiful afternoon when the spring classes commenced. With great confidence, I strode into the classroom, went to the large window overlooking the campus, and provided my first assignment to the waiting students, "Each of you get up and throw your text book out the window."

Following a joint gasp of disbelief, each walked over to the window, and with a gleeful smirk, followed my instructions. I then passed out a copy of Tey's novel with instructions to read the special introduction I provided. This provided me the necessary time to rush down the stairs and out to the lawn, quickly collecting the text books before Dr. Boyden or other members of the school administration would learn what I had just done!

When I returned to the classroom, I now had their undivided attention. "While you have worked hard with the textbook, I know how unexciting this subject can be. At times I was bored, and if I was bored, I know you were bored. So let's try a little experiment."

We then discussed the concept of the historical novel they were about to read, and the change in curriculum they were about to experience. We would spend the next month on a single subject – Richard III. In the process, we would research together, review available material and debate the subject, with the goal being a clear consensus by the class on the controversy. Now I had their attention.

I knew I was taking a risk and within days could easily find myself in Dr. Boyden's office attempting to explain my odd behavior. However, I had already decided not to pursue a teaching career, and would be starting a management program with Pan Am at the end of the school year. So what did I have to lose? And I remembered Dr. Boyden's recurring comment during the spring term when I was a student, "Finish up strong, boys!" And that is what I intended to do, albeit as a teacher.

The next month was a great success, with each class full of enthusiastic students debating the issues. Together we reviewed Sir Thomas More's writings on Richard, and discussed in detail Shakespeare's classic play, Richard III, as a major inspiration for the accepted history of the murdering king. In the end, each student had his own strong opinion on the subject - leading to a clear lack of consensus among the class, although all appeared to have enjoyed and learned from the verbal battles that took place.

In time, the word spread through the campus grapevine about Mr. Broughan's fun class, and I would get "high fives" from fellow teachers envious of the success of my risk-taking. I was succeeding in moving from the mediocrity of rote teaching to bringing history to life and challenging the students' perception of learning. For me it was a victory, proving I could personally do better, and create among my group of young scholars a desire to study more history in the future.

In the final weeks of the school year we went back to the textbook with renewed interest in completing the course. For the final exam, instead of the traditional multi-question test, I asked the students to answer one question in detail, "Was Richard III the evil, murderous monarch depicted by popular history and literature?" Each well-reasoned essay made it evident that I had succeeded in increasing their interest in history, and I would complete my short-lived teaching career with success and a sense of satisfaction. A minor triumph, perhaps, but a triumph nonetheless.

As I moved on to a career in travel that enjoyable spring of 1965, I took valuable lessons from my brief tenure on the Deerfield faculty. Never accept mediocrity in any thing you do, and realize your enthusiasm can be contagious in influencing others – whether at work or play.

For this small, early triumph, I will always be grateful to Dr. Boyden, Josephine Tey, and, most importantly, the erroneously vilified, Richard III.

Pan Am's "Man on the Go!"

ONE COLD AND WINTRY New England morning, I woke up and made a decision. It was time to get a real job - and see the world.

It was early February of 1965, and I was teaching medieval history and coaching at Deerfield Academy in western Massachusetts. Though enjoying the experience and benefiting from the few post grad courses I was taking at nearby University of Massachusetts, it had become clear that this comfortable life was not my future. It was time to fly!

Now that the decision not to pursue a career in academia was made, a new direction was needed. Didn't I say I wanted to see the world? I wanted to fly? Then, obviously, I should seek a career with an airline. And, more specifically, with an international one at that. After all, air travel was still a relatively young industry with plenty of growth opportunities in management. Enthusiastically, letters flew from my typewriter announcing my availability, resulting in total silence as winter became spring, and lacrosse replaced basketball as the major afternoon activity on campus.

Undeterred, my one-way correspondence continued with the major U.S. air carriers. Finally, in early summer, just to stop the annoyance of my prose, I received a positive response from Trans World Airlines, inviting me to an interview at their world headquarters located in a hangar at New York's LaGuardia Airport. They even sent me a ticket to fly from Hartford to LaGuardia on their daily DC 6 service. I was sure this easy one-day trip would ultimately lead to my acceptance of a management position preferably in London or Paris! As I boarded the TWA plane that summer morning (the second flight of my life), little did I realize that this 45-minute flight would be the beginning of millions of miles flown over the next forty years.

My late morning interview with a small team of TWA sales executives was a disaster. It was clear that I did not particularly like these individuals or the opportunity they offered me, and it appeared that they liked me even less. It was now noon and since I was near the Big Apple with no future ahead, what should I do?

I remembered that my unanswered correspondence to Pan American World Airways had been addressed to their new 58-floor skyscraper in mid town Manhattan. And, since TWA was kind enough to give me a lift to New York, why not check in with the world's largest international airline while in town? A quick subway ride to Grand Central Station, followed by a few escalators to the lobby found me in the imposing Pan Am Building.

The directory indicated that the employment office was located on the third floor. Once there, I introduced myself to a disinterested receptionist and advised her that I was seeking employment, specifically in a management position, perhaps in Paris or Hawaii. After kindly advising me that no jobs were currently available, and that I could check back sometime when I was in the area, I explained that I had specifically flown to New York for an interview. She did offer (probably in hopes of quickly getting rid of me) that Pan Am did have a management training program, but that it was incredibly difficult to earn a spot as only one applicant out of hundreds – perhaps thousands - of recent college graduates was accepted on a monthly basis. She mentioned that I could write and send a resume to the executive in charge, Mr. Hardy Dillard.

"Is he located here in the building?" I asked.

"Yes, he has an office on the 52nd floor. But it is impossible to meet with him until your application and resume are reviewed. Even then I am told the waiting list for one of the monthly positions is at least two or more years." the receptionist advised.

Thanking her for the information and with Mr. Dillard's name in hand, I found a bank of express elevators to the 52nd floor. Roaming the halls around the large and impressive executive suites, I happened to pass a small inside office where a young "twenty-something" man was sitting, with his shoes the only items on the desk and reading a *Playboy* magazine. I looked at the nameplate near the door. It read, "Hardy Dillard." Bingo!

"Excuse me, Mr. Dillard, may I bother you for a moment."

"I guess," he replied while laying aside his impressive reading material, "but who are you?"

I quickly explained I was presently teaching at Deerfield Academy, but I was currently seeking a management position with an airline and I had been informed that he was the man I needed to meet.

"Deerfield is a great school. I had several friends at the University of Virginia who went there." A foot in the door.

This initial exchange led to a lengthy conversation about mutual friends at Georgetown and UVA as he had graduated a year before me. It turned out that Hardy's father, a true Virginia gentleman, was a best friend of Pan Am's Senior Vice President, Willis Lipscomb – ah, the plot thickens. We continued talking for an hour about anything and everything other than Pan Am. Then Hardy looked up and asked if I could start the management program the next month! Due to my commitment to Deerfield, I explained that I could not start until after January.

Thus, my career with Pan American Airways commenced on February 1st, and for the next six months I took courses in geography, the make-up of affinity groups, fare construction and other subjects I would never need or use once assigned to a sales position in one of Pan Am's district sales offices in the U.S. I most enjoyed working on special projects for the Executive V.P., or, better yet, the week in London reviewing cargo services at Heathrow Airport when Hardy did not know what else to do with me.

Finally, as the completion of my "strenuous" executive training was coming to an end in mid-summer, Hardy took me to lunch and advised that I had been assigned to the San Francisco sales office. To say I was excited would be an understatement. Pan Am's gateway to Asia was definitely a "plum" assignment, and living on the other coast was exactly what I had hoped for!

A few days later I was called to the office of the V. P. of North American Sales to receive my marching orders and his best wishes.

"You have done a fine job here, and I am confident you will do well working for Bill Schmuck in our Chicago office."

"Bill Schmuck?" "Chicago?" I stammered. "I'm sorry, but I have been assigned to San Francisco," I corrected him.

"I'm sorry but last night we had a change in plans and you have been assigned to Chicago. It's a great office and a fine city. Best of luck to you."

Departing the V.P's office with my newly printed "Man on the Go" introductory brochure in hand, and in a state of shock, I made my way to the third floor ticketing office to obtain what I thought would be a one-way ticket from New York to Chicago on a $40 partner pass using American Airlines. Instead I received two tickets, the first leaving New York the following evening on an overnight flight from JFK to London, with the second ticket for a morning connecting flight from London to Chicago. And so my travel career began – not with a bang, but with a whimper.

Call it luck, or call it karma! Though I always thought Chicago was a place you flew over to get to the west coast, I soon fell in love with the city. I thoroughly enjoyed my job traveling in my "cool" '64 Mustang through the corn fields of Illinois while working with Pan Am's top travel agents. And I really liked my boss with the unlikely name of Schmuck! My free time was even better, making great friends, living in a brownstone on Chicago's Gold Coast with Butch McGuire's Pub on lively Rush Street a few blocks away. It was a short walk to Wrigley Field to watch the Cubs on warm summer days and the Bears on cold and blustery fall Sundays. (Yes, in those days the Bears really did play their home games at Wrigley.)

But most importantly, a joyful, pretty Irish lass named Winnie Moran started working at Pan Am shortly after my arrival – and the rest is history! But that's another story (or chapter).

Pan Am's "Future President"

Day at the Races

LIVING IN CHICAGO IN the late 60's was special if you were a sports fan. Wrigley Field was a short walk or ride on the "L" and tickets for the sunny bleachers were only 75 cents to watch the lovable, losing Cubs.

And every fall, three friends and I had season tickets to enjoy watching the Bears play football at that same Wrigley Field. Then there were the Blackhawks and Bulls playing hockey and basketball at the Chicago Stadium during the winter. The one sporting event I had not taken advantage of since arriving in Chicago, however, was the "Sport of Kings," even though the nearby Arlington Park offered one of the top tracks in the country, with a popular season of racing every summer.

One of my co-workers at International Travel Service, Jack Winkeljohn, lived near the park in Arlington Heights, so he and his wife, Dodie, were enthusiastic regulars. He assured me that we would have a great afternoon if I and my new girlfriend wanted to join them. In fact, the famed Arlington Cup is being held that following Saturday – a perfect opportunity to enjoy horse racing at its best. So the date was set.

On a beautiful, sunny late summer morning, I arrived at Winnie's home in my awesome new canary yellow Oldsmobile Cutlass convertible, and with the top down and hair blowing in the wind, we arrived at the park to meet up with the Winkeljohns. Instead of heading for the $2.00 General Admission grandstand entrance, Jack informed me they had reserved a table with other friends at the prestigious Post and Paddock Club, a much better venue to enjoy the races, especially with the sold-out crowd expected for the Cup Race later that afternoon. "Great," I said, while thinking to myself, what is this unexpected luxury going to cost?

In fact, the $8.00 per person cost seemed reasonable and since I was obviously paying for my date, I quickly calculated that with the $20.00

bill I had with me for the day, I would be left with $4.00 for beverages and betting. Not a good start. Once seated and able to appreciate the outstanding view of the beautiful racetrack on a perfect summer afternoon, I quickly reviewed my strategy for the remainder of the day with that miniscule $4.00 burning a hole in my pocket. First step was to take Winnie aside and sheepishly explain my dilemma asking if I could borrow sufficient funds to buy us each a beer. Being a good sport, she immediately agreed, giving me the opportunity to place a $2.00 bet on the first race, and then prepare to lose my last two dollars on a Daily Double bet. Once this "donation" was given to the track, I planned to carefully nurse my solitary beer the remainder for the afternoon while enjoying all nine races.

I should add here, I knew little to nothing about betting on the horses. While I had previously enjoyed a few days at a track in Maryland with college friends years ago, I never made a dime on the few bets I made on those occasions. Now, looking over *The Racing Form* I borrowed from Jack, along with a few suggestions based on his vast experience in beating the odds, I was off to the betting window with my $4.00 to place my two bets for the day. I should note that I did not follow Winnie's suggested strategy of picking horses based on the color of the jockey's outfit. To further insure a loss of those bets, I selected a horse with twenty to one odds. You can then imagine my shock and total delight while watching this nag confidently fly over the finish line in first place. I literally ran back to the window to collect $29.50. Greatly relieved, I was now set to buy our beers and would even have a few bucks to make additional "winning" bets on some of the later races.

With the running of the second race, the second half of the Daily Double, guess who won? My horse, first again! Not only was I "racing" to collect the winnings from the second race, but also from the Daily Double. The smile and smugness on my face was clearly evident when I returned to the table with more than $100.00 in my pocket, and immediately prepared to lay another $2.00 bet on the third race, which featured a Quinella. To be honest, I didn't even know what a Quinella was, but quickly discovered it was a bet on selecting the two horses that were first to cross the finish line in either first or second place. Compared to the Daily Double, I thought that this option seemed like a snap. So back to the window to make one

$2.00 bet on the horse to win and another $2.00 on the two horses to win the Quinella. You might have guessed what happened. Correct, I won both bets and headed back to collect another $60.00.

For the fourth race there was nothing complicated, simply a $2.00 bet on a horse to win. I selected the favorite, who did win, and I returned with a small but very acceptable $10.00 bill to add to my somewhat bulging pocket of cash.

It was now mid afternoon and I was on my third beer. The fifth race offered a Perfecta – picking the number one and two horses in order as they crossed the finish line. Without hesitation or fear I headed back to the window to place a $2.00 bet on my choice to win and another $2.00 on the Perfecta. Even I was amazed as I walked up to collect another $70.00 for winning both! As I gleefully returned to our group, I noticed that everyone in the Post and Paddock Club was looking at me. The word from our table was that I had won all five races, plus the Daily Double, Quinella and Perfecta – unheard of, as I was to learn.

The sixth race continued my string of successes, and I was now up more than $300.00. The seventh race also featured a Quinella, and again I bet on the horse that won, and also chose the second finisher, winning my second Quinella. So did most of those in the Club, as our table shared my choices with the crowd, and as in all forms of gambling, you go with a "hot hand."

It was now time for the eighth race, the all important Arlington Cup. I headed for the betting window with my $2.00 – followed by most of the people in the room who were continuing to bet along with me. The only exception was my date, who still insisted on choosing her favorite color and refused to follow the crowd, displaying her independence. Unbelievably, I selected the winner to the delight of the entire room, (except, of course, my date, who again picked the wrong color). With more than $400.00 buried in both pockets, I was walking around with more cash than I have ever had in my life.

It was time to make my selection for the ninth and final race, which was also a Perfecta. Confidently selecting and sharing my picks, I headed to the betting window to place my final bets, having now become a "legend" at Arlington. And this time, even Winnie could not resist and she followed my lead.

Ten minutes later my two horses came in dead last. (That clearly should have been an omen for my new girlfriend and future - always independent - wife.)

As we drove to a nearby bar to celebrate my success with the Winkeljohns and their friends, I could hardly contain my excitement. I started planning all the sensible things I would do with these unexpected winnings, like buying the new suit I desperately needed for work. Instead, in my exuberance, I ended up buying a round or two for the entire bar as we discussed my success that afternoon at Arlington. Later that evening, with a significantly diminished portion of my vast winnings in hand, we drove back to Chicago with the top down, enjoying a balmy evening and talking about that special day I would likely tell to anyone patient enough to listen to the tale – including you just now!

On Monday, Jack told the entire office of my adventure and subsequent new-found wealth suggesting that I take everyone to lunch. When that idea was quickly rejected due to insufficient funds, he advised that he was returning to the track that evening. Greedily, I checked the *Chicago Tribune* and gave him $2.00 to bet on the Daily Double that night. I won. When he gave me my winnings the next morning, he suggested we go to the track together every night that week. I declined, deciding I would go out on top. Now, some 45 years later, I have never been back to the races!

A "Fourth" to Remember
(and an Anniversary Hard to Forget)

"**I**T SHOULD BE A Saturday in the summer since my two sisters are teachers," I announced. Without a moment's hesitation, she consulted her memorized 1970 calendar, and with a twinkle in her eye replied, "How about July 4th?"

We were lingering on the dance floor at the annual Pan Am Christmas Party following a slow song, the only kind I was capable of dancing without making a total fool of myself. And as romantic as I am sure it sounds, I had unexpectedly proposed to Winnie and she had obviously accepted during that thirty-second repartee that would change our lives.

Later that Friday night, after dropping her off at her "geographically undesirable" home on Chicago's north side, I finally had time to review what I had just done. While still in shock, I realized the next step required a more proper and formal proposal as one would expect from a Jesuit-trained gentleman. So off I rushed to Tiffany's with a diamond ring Nana had given me a few years ago, perhaps thinking ahead to this occasion. Her second husband, Jack, wore it with pride until he passed away and Nana knew it would be the perfect engagement ring for my future bride.

Two weeks later, on a snowy but festive New Year's Eve, we enjoyed a cocktail at the elegant Prince of Wales lounge in the Ambassador East Hotel where the Tiffany set engagement ring was presented to my future bride as I officially asked for her hand in marriage.

A day later the rush was on! The Moran's neighborhood church, St. Matthias, was booked for our wedding mass, with the reception set for the ballroom at the Orrington Hotel in nearby Evanston for July 4th, 1970. I do not need to go into the gory details of the work and planning required for the "Big Event." Thankfully, Winnie, an event planner at heart, took full responsibility for the myriad of details while I spent the better part of the winter and spring traveling on business. (The poor girl should have clearly seen the torturous path she would follow for many years into the future.)

For my part, I had only one responsibility – to find us a place to live starting July 1st. Perhaps another clear omen for Winnie was my total lack of success with that single assignment as May came and went, and our wedding now a mere month away. With the pressure mounting, I started checking the weekend *Chicago Tribune* rental listings in the wee hours each Friday morning knowing I had to be the first in line when the right apartment presented itself.

And voila! There it was one morning in early June – a one-bedroom apartment in the heart of Lincoln Park, the exact area where we wanted to live. The only problem was the cost, $260.00 a month, well over our budget. But budgets have never stopped me, so I left at daybreak to meet our new landlords. David and Felice Reiter welcomed me and provided a tour of THE perfect apartment, necessitating my most professional sales performance - begging them for the lease with tears in my eyes, explaining that my marriage and my future was now in their hands. Later that day they confirmed that the apartment was ours. (They were both wonderful and unusual landlords, especially since our rent never changed during the idyllic seven years we lived there.) With my sole assignment successfully completed three weeks prior to the "big day," it was time to party and enjoy those final days of bachelorhood, which, indeed, I did.

July quickly arrived – as did one of the most oppressive heat waves in recent memory. Our friends and my family arrived in Chicago to experience temperatures of 100 plus with equally high humidity. The fourth-floor walk up grey stone apartment I shared with Lou Gonzales was in a word, unbearable. So Lou, my Chimes friends in the wedding party, Kevin O'Brien, Perry Butler, Bill Casey and I spent the better part of those last two days in the air-conditioned comfort of Butch McGuire's Pub. This included my bachelor party in Butch's private basement office – clearly indicating what a loyal client I had been the last few years!

The rehearsal at St. Matthias the evening of the 3rd was followed by dinner for our families at the Moran house a few blocks from the church. During the two block walk from the church, Winnie's father provided me with some sound advice on my intention to marry his only child – "You're making a big mistake, you know!" (Clearly Tom missed those nights in the local pubs enjoying pints with his old friends. Thankfully, he was definitely wrong.)

In the middle of that night a minor miracle occurred, the incredible hot and humid weather was replaced by a crisp, cool, sunny, beautiful summer day - the perfect sign that this fateful day was to be enjoyed, and indeed it was. First, by having a final burger and pint with friends at Melvin's, a neighborhood favorite for the past five years. Then, later that afternoon, on entering the side door of the church, awaiting the initial notes of "Greensleeves," and Winnie's walk down the aisle to the altar. To be honest, about the only thing I remember about the wedding mass, itself, was how nervous, but excited I was. Those faded black and white photos in the wedding album, however, clearly indicate that the marriage did happen – as did the lively reception that evening. (Including a fireworks display provided by the city of Evanston, obviously in our honor.)

We did not get much sleep that night in our suite at the Drake Hotel on Chicago's lakefront. We made the mistake of inviting our friends back to the hotel for a nightcap and they enthusiastically accepted – for multiple nightcaps, in fact. So, when we finally saw the light of another beautiful summer day, it was time to head to O'Hare Airport and our Pan Am flight to Shannon for our planned week-long honeymoon in Ireland and London.

Upon check-in we were advised that the First Class section of the Boeing 707 aircraft was being reserved exclusively for us, and once the flight was airborne, a champagne bottle was popped prior to our multi-course dinner. Already, I was loving marriage. Some of our friends thought it was great idea to order a bottle of champagne and have it presented to us on our flight to take with us to enjoy during our honeymoon. The complication was that six different friends came up with the same excellent idea. I wish I now had a photo of me deplaning in Shannon attempting to carry all six bottles in my arms to our honeymoon castle, Dromoland, an actual 16th century castle near Shannon.

After months of planning and preparing and then the last few days of celebrating, we were ready for a long nap once happily ensconced in our magnificent turret suite. Little did I realize that the nap would last all three days we stayed in Dromoland. Winnie was truly exhausted. She slept, leaving me ample opportunity to take care of the bottles of champagne we were meant to enjoy. The only way to wake her was to whisper in the early evening, "Fresh Irish salmon now being served." Once the salmon was enjoyed, the head was back on the pillow, while I enjoyed yet another bottle of the bubbly stuff. Once rested, however, we enjoyed visits to family homes in Mayo, including the home of Winnie's parents in Newport. (Not realizing another Newport directly across the ocean would become our home more than thirty years later.)

It is a coincidence that I am writing of these memorable days in July in our Newport home, exactly 47 years since we stood before family and friends committing to be together forever. Now 16,425 days later we are continuing that commitment while enjoying each and every day! Bring on day 20,000 – We are not done doing!

Waiting for the Fireworks

A Special Relationship,
Lasting Half a Century

"**L**OOK AT THAT SNOW," said a gloomy Ted Toay, "and they say it will continue through most of the night. I seriously doubt we will be leaving for Hawaii tomorrow morning."

Ted and I were both relatively new sales reps for Pan Am in Chicago, and we had been invited on a four day familiarization visit to Kona on the Big Island of Hawaii. We were scheduled to depart the next morning and things were looking dim.

"I bet they can plow before morning." I replied, "So we will be out of this snow, and sipping Mai Tais while enjoying a Kona sunset tomorrow afternoon." The fact that I had to abandon my '65 green mustang a few blocks from my Astor Street apartment because of the heavy snow drifts should have provided a dose of reality to my morning traffic plans as the falling snow was rapidly becoming a blizzard Chicago would talk about for years to come. In spite of the obvious, I refused to accept the inevitable. After all, this would be my first visit to Hawaii, and how many chances would I have in lifetime to experience the islands that everyone I knew considered to be paradise. Warm weather all year, with tropical breezes, friendly people who offered a welcoming "Aloha" to all visitors, hulas, luaus and magnificent sandy beaches. Hawaii had it all – and I wanted it, if only for four days.

As the snow continued to fall, and my Mustang now totally covered in an ever-growing snow bank, I prepared for my Hawaiian mini vacation by enjoying another delightful evening with friends at Butch McGuire's Pub, a few short blocks from my apartment. Early the next morning I awoke to a clear sky, increasing my confidence that the flight to Hawaii would be on schedule. With my suitcase in hand, I walked out the front door of our building and down the stairs in search of a taxi to O'Hare

Airport. As I hit the street, the snow was up to my waist and the eerie silence confirmed that I would not be sipping Mai Tais that evening – at least not in Hawaii.

The good news, however, was that the Kona Visitor's Bureau still wanted us to visit and rescheduled the trip. So, a few weeks later Ted and I departed for a wonderful four days in paradise.

In the late winter of 1966, Kona was a small village compared to the state capital of Honolulu on the island of Oahu, but as far as I was concerned, nothing could have been better. Hawaii easily exceeded my expectations during this brief encounter and I was anxious to return some-day. Little did I realize I would return to Hawaii well over one hundred times during the next half century and would enjoy each and every visit.

Many of the trips were all business, working with incentive groups, conventions and corporate meetings, initially when working for International Travel Service in Chicago, and later with Group Travel Unlimited, when I became president of this large convention coordination company located in Washington, DC in 1979. Later business visits were in conjunction with planning for and operating the cruises of the S.S. *Monterey* in the Hawaiian Islands in the late 80s. But the best visits were the relaxing and memorable family vacations where together we experienced the best of all the islands.

In the last few years, our retirement has allowed Winnie and I extended stays in recent winters, and through it all, Hawaii always remains a special place – one that combines a natural beauty with an atmosphere that emanates from the Hawaiian's natural spirit of "Aloha."

With so many memories of these visits to this special place, it is appropriate for me to "talk story" as the Hawaiians say that might both entertain as well as help to appreciate why the islands have been so special to me over many years.

A GULLIBLE WINNIE

"I'm not kidding, a $10,000 investment will be worth a half million dollars in less than 10 years." I advised my brand new adorable wife – using my best salesmanship approach to the topic.

The subject at hand was an opportunity to acquire a fully furnished one bedroom condominium at the recently completed Maui Eldorado, located along the front nine of the Ka'anapali Championship Golf Course, overlooking the blue Pacific and the majestic mountains of the islands of Lanai and Molokai. There could not be a more perfect setting for any visitor to the beautiful island of Maui.

I had just returned from a business trip to Hawaii escorting attendees to the annual convention of the America Society of Obstetricians and Gynecologists. Winnie and I had been married for less than a year, and I was still working for International Travel Service in Chicago. The convention was held in Honolulu, and following those meetings I lead a smaller group of doctors on a five night tour to Maui and Kona.

During our three nights at the sprawling Maui Hilton, the association had organized a full day of medical sessions, so the good doctors could legitimately claim a tax deduction of their travel expenses. Enjoying the free day, I decided to walk across the golf course to visit a model apartment at Maui Eldorado, not yet fully realizing that the easiest sale for any salesman is to make his pitch to another salesman. After an hour I was hooked. It was easy to envision the future popularity of Maui, and especially this under-developed Ka'anapali Beach Resort area. I firmly believed that owning a prime apartment with an unmatched view of the golf course, ocean and nearby islands would be the investment of a lifetime. The only problem was I had no savings and my $22,000 a year salary was just enough to cover our less-than-extravagant lifestyle in our one-bedroom Lincoln Park apartment.

On my return flight to Chicago at the end of the tour, I remembered that Winnie did have a special savings account slightly in excess of the magical $10,000 needed to purchase the condo – the key to our financial future. All the way back to Chicago I worked on my very best sales pitch to present to my wife and soon-to-be business partner. A few weeks later, with check in hand, we headed to Maui for a week-long vacation and a final inspection of what would become our first – and last - vacation home.

Even Winnie, while much more conservative and realistic than myself, was impressed with the condo and its potential. Her greatest concern was the possible overbuilding of the pristine Ka'anapali Resort, but I assured her that the developers would not allow such a problem. Perhaps one or two more low standing hotels would be constructed along the extensive pristine beachfront, but nothing to destroy the intrinsic beauty of the area. To prove how knowledgeable I was, one only needs to sit on a Maui Eldorado lanai today to view miles of hotels and high rise condominiums "cheek to jowl" along not only Ka'anapali Beach itself, but for the ten miles of coastline stretching all the way north to Kapalua, which at the time of our purchase was a very rural area full of pineapples and sugarcane.

To insure our financial success, we developed a business plan to rent out the condo to friends and strangers, which included producing our own brochure, complete with photos and our "expert prose" pointing out the benefits of our perfect vacation offering. Whenever anyone asked me "as a travel professional" where I would recommend going for a perfect vacation, the answer never varied – and Maui Eldorado D204 had another happy guest.

As part of our ownership responsibilities, we felt it was a requirement to make tax-deductible visits to our business venture every six months or so, to make sure that all was in order. Oh, how we loved these business trips!

For more than a year and a half we continued to rent D204. While we were just covering our costs, I continued to believe the value of our apartment would escalate. In fact, developers were just starting to build north in Kapalua and south in Wialea.

"Just think," I explained to Winnie, "if we only had $20,000 more we could buy one condo in each of these new resorts, and in ten years the three would be worth more than a million dollars."

"Dream on," was her response. Well, indeed, it was a dream.

In 1972 the United States, and especially Hawaii, was hit with an oil crisis, and our maintenance costs quickly escalated. At the same time it became clear that, although my vision might be "brilliant," our finances did not match my brilliance.

That year we sold D204 to a wealthy Texan for $75,000, and he immediately renovated it and turned it into a real second home. So, our first – and most enjoyable - investment came to an end.

And now for the rest of the story! A number of years later, I escorted another convention group to Maui. In that short period of time, it was hard to believe how development on the island had expanded. Maui had quickly become a major vacation destination for visitors worldwide. During a free afternoon my curiosity got the best of me, and I headed to the Maui Eldorado Sales Office to see how our first investment was doing. There was a similar one-bedroom unit available for resell, but without the exceptional view of D204, and it was being sold unfurnished. The asking price was $620,000!

A visionary? Perhaps. A real estate tycoon? Not!

Kona Fisherman

Members of the previously mentioned Society of Obstetricians and Gynecologists continued with their Hawaiian tour to the resort town of Kona on the Island of Hawaii. During our time in Honolulu and Maui I had become friends with a couple from San Diego. He was a devoted deep sea fisherman – in fact he had his own fishing boat berthed at San Diego Harbor. At the time, Kona was well known as a destination for Marlin fishing.

My doctor friend had chartered a fishing vessel prior to our arrival in Kona, and he invited me to join him and his wife for a day at sea. I was very excited as I had never previously experienced this exciting sport.

It was a beautiful morning as we left the Kona pier, although the ocean was choppy and likely to get worse, according to our young captain. He was correct, and an hour later our experienced fisherman and his wife were below deck suffering from a rather severe bout of sea sickness.

Thankfully, I was not yet afflicted so I joined the captain to trawl for the boat's catch. In a short period of time, my line became taught and I soon became the proud owner of a forty-foot blue marlin. I yelled down to my friends to tell them of our good fortune. They were not particularly impressed.

Less than a half an hour later my line tightened even more aggressively. Twenty minutes later the captain and I were hauling in an even larger (almost 80 pounds) cousin of our first catch. The captain could not believe it. "You know how many times experienced deep sea fishermen have spent days out here and have never caught a thing? Here you are – never fished before, and you have two trophies?"

My friends below are still not impressed.

"Perhaps we should head back in" I offered. In agreement now, our quite pleased captain headed to shore while leaving the two large fishing rods in their stands with the lines still trolling. It could not have been five minutes before a tug so strong almost pulled one of the rods into the sea, slowing the boat. The captain joined me and a huge, exhausting battle at sea had begun. Thanks to the experience and stamina of the captain, we – "together" – eventually pulled in a two-hundred-forty pound black marlin.

"This has to be the largest catch of the winter, and I am calling ahead to spread the news. Let's pull in the lines and head for shore," announced my excited, though exhausted leader.

My friends, in spite of their condition, were now impressed!

As we pulled up to the dock a team had gathered to help lift and weigh my (our) trophy catch. Indeed, it was the largest catch of the season. (School children on the island would be enjoying tasty fish sticks for weeks to come.) The local Kona newspaper even sent a reporter and photographer to document the haul.

The doctor and his wife had recovered sufficiently to be photographed with the large magnificent creature, so, at least, they earned that photo memory for the money spent.

Later that evening over cocktails at the Kona Hilton, he told me that in twenty years of fishing the California coast, he had never experienced such an unbelievable catch. Clearly, I must be a natural deep sea fisherman!

I have never gone deep sea fishing since!

DeKalb

My first major achievement in the incentive travel business featured Hawaii, though, actually, it was initiated a half a world away in Madrid, Spain.

International Travel Service was appointed to coordinate travel for the American delegates to the World Poultry Federation in the summer of 1973. My role was to design and escort a pre-conference incentive to the coastal resort of Marbella, Spain for the Poultry Division of DeKalb

Ag Research. It was a small, intimate group, and all had a most enjoyable time, showering me with compliments as we headed to Madrid and the actual World Conference.

In fact, the manager of the Poultry Division, who was both feared and apparently disliked by all but his wife, children and dog, took a liking to me. "You know, our small group is peanuts," he said, when we met in the lobby of the Palace Hotel in Madrid one night. "It's our main seed division that has the big bucks to pay for large incentive trips for the top dealers."

"Could you set up a meeting for me?" I asked.

"I am sure I could, but I will tell you now, you would not have a chance in hell of getting the business. The heads of that division are in bed with Harry Redman and that E.F. McDonald team in Dayton."

I was well aware of Redman and McDonald's. They were the "eight hundred pound gorilla" in the industry, running thousands of trips each year for most of the top Fortune 100 companies in the U.S. In fact, Redman was a legend in the business. To take away a lucrative account like DeKalb, the country's largest seed business, would be like Daniel slaying Goliath in the incentive travel industry.

Upon our return to Chicago, I pursued an appointment with the marketing team of that same Seed Division. After an initial meeting, they decided to allow ITS to bid, and a few weeks later they provided specifications for a four-night trip to Honolulu the following December for some 4,000 dealers throughout the Midwest and Southwest. To this day, I firmly believe they thought they were simply providing pricing competition for the McDonald group to keep them honest.

Following the submission of our proposal, I was summoned to the headquarters in DeKalb, Illinois to make a final presentation of our proposal to a large team of DeKalb's sales and marketing executives. To say I was nervous would be an understatement!

For years, as I traveled throughout Illinois as a Pan Am sales rep, I saw those flying ears of corn logos everywhere. I understood just how big this company was. I also knew that they realized ITS and I had never operated an incentive trip for more than 100 participants. Why would they possibly take a chance with our firm?

"You have offered the lowest bid," advised their Incentive Manager, Leo Damkroger, "but McDonald's is offering the best hotel in Honolulu, the Hilton Hawaiian Village – while you have selected the Ala Moana, which we have never heard of."

It took my very best sales effort to show why their dealers would enjoy a brand new deluxe hotel overlooking the Ala Moana Shopping Center instead of the beautiful beach front location offered by Hilton. Even I had a hard time swallowing as I laid out the "benefits" – most importantly a huge savings to the company if it worked.

"McDonald has handled larger groups than ours regularly. But your company has had very little experience with groups as large as ours," the Incentive Manager said.

"We certainly have operated large conventions successfully, and, to be honest, they are more challenging to coordinate and the individual clients are more demanding," I responded. "Plus, we are hungrier for your business so we are prepared to offer DeKalb a better value and will give each of your dealers a more personalized experience before and during the actual trip."

A week later, I and the entire ITS team was shocked to learn we had been awarded the business. The only people who were possibly more shocked were Harry Redman and his E.F. McDonald team. There was also shock among the travel industry executives in Hawaii who knew ITS as a meeting coordinator but not as an incentive travel specialist.

So this was my 'home run!' The DeKalb account would allow me and ITS to take a place as players in the incentive travel business – and a potential key player in the Hawaiian Market!

Now the real work began. First came the negotiation for four United airlines DC8s, carrying 950 DeKalb dealers back-to-back on four rotations for a total of 3,800 guests in Honolulu over a 16-day period. A bigger issue remained however; will the new Ala Moana Hotel really work? Will the dealers grumble at being at a shopping center rather than in the elegant new Hilton Rainbow Tower directly on Waikiki Beach? Before leaving for Honolulu on the planning visit, I decided to make contact with Bob Moore, the Director of Sales at the Hilton. Early December was traditionally one of the lowest seasons of the year in Hawaii. I took a chance to see how much he wanted the business.

Upon arrival at Honolulu International Airport, I was met by a private limousine driver, hired to take me to the Ala Moana, compliments of Mr. Moore and the Hilton Hawaiian Village. I had my answer! But the big question was working together, could we make the numbers fit my tight budget – that would be the challenge.

The following morning Bob and I met, toured the hotel, negotiated for a few hours and agreed to work together hosting the DeKalb dealers at the Hilton. My job was easy in convincing the DeKalb executives to switch from the Ala Moana to the deluxe beachfront Hilton. Bob's job was more difficult, as he had to explain that he lowered his price for ITS. However 400 room nights for sixteen days in early December was too good to pass up.

The actual operation of the onslaught of farmers that December was a great success. The dealers enjoyed their brief visit and the DeKalb executives were most pleased with the effort of the ITS staff. In fact, we had such a large staff; I had little to do during the sixteen days. That allowed me to enjoy many late evenings at the Ilikai Hotel listening to Loyal Garner, one of Hawaii's best entertainers, known as Hawaii's "Lady of Love." She was a magnet for all of the island's top stars, like Don Ho, who would often join her after their own shows. Those evenings were "the best of times" for Hawaiian entertainment.

There was a special individual on the island of Maui, however, who did not have it quite so easy. In fact, she was facing a real challenge given her by an overly creative husband. Winnie was the sole host to the top DeKalb managers in a program designed by "yours truly" to tax the most experienced travel professional.

As part of the DeKalb incentive plan, the company's top sales managers and their wives flew with their dealers to serve as hosts during the stay at the Hilton. DeKalb then rewarded them with an additional four nights of R&R. When asked for my recommendation for this extension, I selected my favorite island, Maui, of course. Also, rather than a boring hotel resort there (the type of accommodation that E.F. McDonald would have selected) I recommended a condo style vacation at, you guessed it, Maui Eldorado.

The executives were intrigued. Each manager would have a one-bedroom suite with a full kitchen, and all suites have incredible views of the Pacific and the nearby islands of Lanai and Molokai. In addition, they would have use of Eldorado's private beach club on Ka'anapali Beach, plus their own rental cars for personal sightseeing. We would also fill the refrigerators in each unit with fresh fruits, breakfast foods and beverages, including beer and wine. Each night they would enjoy dinner at one of Maui's best restaurants. And one night there would be a sunset cocktail party at the exclusive beach club. In brief, an exciting and creative concept.

The only problem, since the Eldorado was a condo development, it had no hotel staff, so our personally selected escort and host for this exclusive program had lots of extra work to do, which would not be required if a traditional hotel had been recommended. For each of the four back-to-back visits, she not only operated the hospitality desk daily to answer questions and help with sightseeing suggestions, but was actively involved in many other "fun" activities in her spare time. Like shopping for all the food and beverages for each of the twenty apartments every four days – completely filling up her small Toyota with multiple grocery bags that then needed to sorted, repacked and delivered to each condo before the arrival of the next group of forty happy DeKalb managers. (It should be noted that the "creative genius" of this effort provided her with a manual Toyota, in spite of the fact that she had no experience driving with a manual shift, causing tears and trepidation at stop signs on the small hills leaving Lahaina after shopping for forty!)

In the evenings, her spare time was cleverly used to make hors d'oeuvres for the cocktail party on the third night of each group's stay. By her own calculations, the Hawaiian Meatballs made and consumed during those sixteen days were counted in the thousands – likely the reason she has never made me any of these favorite snacks the last forty years.

The highlight, however, was the actual cocktail party. For each group, I left my comfortable situation in Honolulu to fly over to the tiny commuter airport at Ka'anapali in time to join the sunset festivities. I was always so glad I did. While Winnie, in her Hawaiian mumu, was racing back and forth across the golf course fairway to get more meatballs or tonic water, she could hear me being congratulated and cheered by the managers and their wives for arranging such a wonderful trip.

"Why did we ever use E.F. McDonald," they would say. "From now on it is John Broughan and ITS!" It did my heart good.

As for Winnie, right then and there she should have known it was going to be a difficult "ride" for the next forty years.

FLYING COMPANIONS

My work in travel related businesses for some forty years provided many memorable experiences and special friendships around the world. Unfortunately, it also meant too many days and nights flying to various global destinations. During those early years there were no movies on demand, iPhones or even laptops for working or entertainment. Instead most fellow travelers were found carrying overstuffed briefcases filled with paperwork to complete during the flight.

Often, however, the most enjoyable time was spent in extended conversations with interesting seat partners. And over many years spent flying in and out of Washington, DC airports, it was inevitable to share a flight with a number of notable Washingtonians, including many congressmen and senators. One such occasion found me sitting directly in front of Senator Ted Kennedy on a short flight to Boston, who loved talking to one and all around him. Conversely, Senator Bill Bradley did chat briefly on a flight to Miami in order to criticize my choice of watch and tie. I thoroughly enjoyed my conversation on an evening flight with Supreme Court Justice William Brennan, a true gentleman.

Not all were politicians, however. One flight on Eastern Airlines left the gate with only one empty seat, next to me in first class. A few minutes later it pulled back to the gate, allowing the late-arriving president of Eastern to board and join me. Frank Borman, an early NASA astronaut and commander of Apollo 8 mission to the moon, was now the President of Eastern Airlines and he provided an fascinating discussion during our short flight to Miami.

An unusual conversation with a member of congress was not actually in flight, but at the Delta Lounge in Salt Lake City. The then junior senator from Utah, Orrin Hatch, came over on crutches to sit beside me while we awaited our flight to DC. While describing his recent skiing accident, we were interrupted by a lounge hostess indicating that the White House was on the phone at the front desk. A few minutes later, Senator Hatch hobbled back and related his brief conversation with President Ronald Reagan, who had called to ask about the senator's recovery. The President offered excellent advice to the senator, explaining that when his own broken arm was in a cast years ago, he used a properly bent wire coat hanger to itch beneath the cast and suggested the senator use the same trick himself. Senator Hatch obviously enjoyed receiving the presidential tip.

Perhaps the most entertaining seatmate was Richard Simmons, well known for his antics on his popular aerobic exercise TV show. He was a great non-stop conversationalist except when he could no longer sit still and needed to stroll up and down the aisle to talk to his many adoring admirers – although given their size they we apparently watchers rather than participants in his non-stop half hour tortures!

One of the most memorable seat mates was on one of the many long flights to and from Hawaii in the mid-eighties. Because of the frequency and length of these trips, I had developed a workable plan to use time wisely. Departing Washington for Los Angeles, I would do some paperwork immediately after take-off, and then enjoy dinner and a few glasses of wine to relax and prepare to sleep on the next leg of the journey from Los Angeles to Hawaii. Once in LA, I enjoyed a little fresh air during a short walk to the TWA Terminal to board a 9:00pm departure where I would nap for a portion of this second flight before a midnight arrival in Honolulu and a short night in a hotel before beginning work the next morning.

On one of these lengthy journeys, I found myself seated in a comfortable window seat on the upper deck of a TWA 747. When a short mechanical delay was announced I decided to commence my nap, and, apparently did not wake during takeoff. In fact, I was sleeping so soundly, my eyes did not open until the Captain advised we would soon fly over the Big Island and he was expecting a landing in Honolulu in approximately 40 minutes. I then heard what sounded like a very familiar voice from the gentleman next to me who must have boarded after I fell asleep, "I am very jealous of your ability to sleep on long flights. I have never been able to do that myself." Looking over at my seat mate to respond, not only did I recognize the voice but the familiar face as well. Walter Cronkite had been my source of national and world news since I was in high school – the very same anchor who delivered details of so many events in my early life, from national conventions, and inaugurations, as well as the unforgettable announcement of JFK's assassination while I was in my senior year at Georgetown. Cronkite, retired from his CBS anchor position, was producing documentaries while also speaking to organizations as he was scheduled to do the following evening in Honolulu. We continued an enjoyable conversation until our arrival at the terminal where he was met by the TWA airport manager and a private driver. Since we were staying at adjacent hotels in Waikiki, he offered me a lift in his limo, so we continued our conversation and sharing our mutual enjoyment of being in Hawaii, even after a long flight.

Though I have told of some of my more notable seat mates here, one of the more enjoyable and enlightening aspects of being a member of the airlines "Million Miler" club was the wide variety of fellow passengers, all in the same boat (or in this case, plane) sharing stories and good conversation on our way toward the next destination – or better yet, home.

THE CRUISE FROM HELL

A T THAT MOMENT I was feeling very good about myself, a modern day Captain Cook, greeting the 170 guests who would be joining me on a cruise they would never forget. We gathered that winter day in the departure lounge at Chicago's O'Hare waiting to board our Pan Am chartered 707 to warm and sunny San Juan where we would embark on our private yacht-like cruise vessel for seven idyllic days in a part of the Caribbean few knew existed.

The cruise industry was in its infancy in the winter of 1971, and the larger ships from Miami all visited the same major islands such as St. Thomas and St. Martin. Our travel company, ITS, focused on group travel and took a different route by chartering smaller vessels where we could chart our own itineraries. During the past two winters we had worked successfully with Epirotiki Cruises, a Greek cruise line and the largest in Europe at the time, as they repositioned their vessels from the inhospitable Aegean Sea to the welcoming Caribbean for the winter season.

For this special cruise, we had selected Epirotiki's smallest vessel, the *S.S. Neptune*, ideal for the 170 passengers waiting to board the Pan Am plane. The *Neptune* was more like a large private yacht than a full size cruise ship providing intimate accommodations. The major attraction for me as the trip organizer was the opportunity to select small, unknown islands in the protected waters of the Grenadines in the lower Eastern Caribbean – in fact, most of the islands we planned to visit had never welcomed a cruise ship crammed with happy vacationers.

A large banner was draped behind the departure desk stating, *Pan Am Welcomes the Illinois Association of Realtors.* I had the pleasure of working with this large state association and traveling with them on chartered trips to Europe the past two winters. So it was like greeting old friends as we boarded our private jet. The four-hour flight passed quickly, thanks to an open bar, and our travelers were whisked from the San Juan airport to the port terminal in a jolly mood, ready to embark on the S.S. *Neptune* and begin our adventure.

The first omen of things to come appeared when I was approached by a couple who had traveled with me previously. "Hey, John, we can't find our cabin – 201." Together we approached the Purser's Desk to discover that, in fact, there was no Cabin 201, contrary to the berthing book provided by Epirotiki and used to assign cabins on this sold-out cruise. Looking at my chart the Purser smugly added, "There is no cabin 202 either, although it looks like you assigned it to the Scotts." I felt a tap on my shoulder and wasn't surprised to see it was Mr. Scott, also looking for his cabin. With every cabin sold and now occupied, my hands began to sweat as the limited options raced through my stressed-out brain. I first offered both couples accommodations for the week at a beach front resort. Or I, along with the other ITS escort, would give up our small single cabins with upper and lower berths if they wanted to stay on board. Both couples opted for the ship, and I was contemplating seven romantic evenings sleeping on a deck chair under a sky of twinkling stars! To make matters worse, I was then accosted by an attractive single woman, who had booked this cruise convinced that it would be the romantic interlude she saw each week on *The Love Boat*. Once onboard, she quickly realized this was no Love Boat, and except for me and our other escort, everyone else were married couples. "Where are the single men – where is the sex?" she shouted. I now knew that this was going to be a very long week!

With all now successfully accommodated, the party that started on the Pan Am flight continued with a Bon Voyage Party on the open deck as our magical yacht pulled out of the harbor and towards the open sea and the straits separating San Juan from the Virgin Islands. Once at sea, the passengers adjourned to the main lounge for my trip announcements prior to the Welcome Dinner in the ship's dining room. As I was speaking, I noticed stewards entering the rear of the lounge holding trays of white boxes, similar to Chinese food take-out cartons. It was at this moment our small vessel encountered serious turbulent currents that are prevalent on leaving San Juan harbor – something neither Epirotiki nor the Captain felt necessary to mention. Within minutes, my eloquent address was overshadowed by guests grabbing the offered boxes as seasickness raced through the lounge while passengers raced to their cabins in an attempt to avoid the inevitable. An hour later, I sat with the Captain and the Cruise Director in a totally empty Dining Room, waiting for the Welcome Dinner that never happened. Somehow, I had a funny feeling about the next seven days – and it wasn't a pretty thought.

The next morning was a life-saver for all on board. We arrived on a small island in the Virgin chain to warm and beautiful weather. After a short visit on land, most recovered from seasickness and the overall mood of the group became enthusiastic. I assured them the following days would be calm sailing as we entered the sheltered Grenadine Islands with ideal cruising conditions for our intimate vessel. And true to my word, after a smooth overnight sail, we awoke to a breathtaking sight as we arrived at the dock on the charming island of Bequia.

When I visited this island previously during the final planning for this cruise, I discovered that the *Neptune* would indeed be the first cruise ship to ever visit, at least during the lifetimes of those islanders I met with. And to make sure our visit was a highlight of our cruise the only school on the island had closed so the children, and, in fact, all residents of the island could greet us. This also enabled us to use the only two buses on the island, school buses, supplemented by trucks loaded with pews from the church, to provide tours for our passengers. The local ladies made island clothing that the passengers could purchase, and Bequia was home to scrimshaw artists who had interesting examples of their art for sale. Our visit was a great success for both our cruisers and the islanders. (Even the single woman looking for love appeared to being enjoying herself!) Late in the afternoon, the *Neptune* set sail for our next adventure on the tiny island of Petite St. Vincent.

On my planning visit, I quickly learned why the island was called "petite" – indeed it was. However it did have one lovely beach resort that accommodated up to twenty couples in high season. So, in designing the itinerary, I decided this port of call would be an ideal destination for an overnight stay where we could plan a special evening – a sunset cocktail party on the large private beach at the resort followed by a barbecue with a lively steel band. The hotel owners agree to host the event, although they were concerned about feeding 170 people at one time – something they had never been called on to do before. No fear, I told them, as realtors loved to drink, they will not mind any delays in serving food so long as libations are at hand.

The *Neptune* docked at the tiny pier of Petite St. Vincent in the early afternoon. Again the only transportation on the island were school buses, put into service to provide tours of this beautiful but isolated island. While the guests were on tour, I headed directly to the hotel for a final check on the evening arrangements. I was enthusiastically met by the owners who offered me a glass of the special rum punch they had prepared for the sunset cocktails. I took a sip and found it to be quite delicious. With the second sip, however, I began to feel lightheaded – as if I had just enjoyed a large martini. When I asked about the recipe, the owners explained that I had told them the Realtors like to drink and party, so they used their special 120 proof island rum in the punch. In a flash, I knew this was going to be some beach party!

And it WAS! The evening, with a beautiful sunset, swimming in the warm ocean and friendly conversation, enhanced by the powerful rum punch, quickly turned into a boisterous, fun-filled event. After dinner, the revelers were even dancing to that lively steel band – even though the band had failed to show up! To my relief, our single woman had joined the fun. She was now laughing and thoroughly enjoying herself; smiling broadly, although she had no teeth, and, worse yet, she was sufficiently inebriated that she did not seem to notice. Apparently, as the evening was drawing to a close, she had gone to the Ladies Room where she needed to unload some of that delicious rum punch she had been enjoying, and in the process had also thrown up her upper and lower dentures. In her current state she proceeded to flush them down the drain. By the time some brave souls had the courage to advise her of her modified appearance, the drowned teeth were floating somewhere in the dark Caribbean Sea. In yet another yelling scene that was both comical and tragic, I was, needless to say, responsible for her condition and what was I going to do about it. As my mind churned, I asked myself, what would Captain Stubing of *The Love Boat* have done? Back on the *Neptune*, the poor woman, victimized by "my punch and party," went to sulk and hide in her cabin while the rest of our rowdy cruisers retired to sleep off the island party that most would not remember the next day.

It was that next day and that next island I had looked forward to the most when selecting the ports of call the year before. Palm Island – mysterious, uninhabited, but boasting the most beautiful crescent-shaped beach of fine white sand and framed by perfectly shaped palm trees. As I previously viewed the available photos of this picturesque island, I could only imagine it somewhere in the most romantic part of the South Pacific. Once again we would be the first cruise to experience its natural beauty. As we approached this untouched, almost perfect image of blue water, white sand and green palm trees, there was not a cloud in the sky and I knew this would be the day our passengers would talk about when they returned home – a full day with a private deserted beach all to ourselves – idyllic!

While gazing on all this natural beauty, there was an announcement, "John Broughan to the bridge." Once there, the captain brusquely informed me that Palm Island was no longer our destination. "The currents are too strong here, the reefs are not clear on my nautical map and the wind is coming from the wrong direction" he explained.

Undeterred, I asked, "Why can't we just anchor?"

"Too deep," he replied, "and possible shallow reefs ahead are too dangerous." Exploring his maps we discovered another island just to the south that might have more favorable conditions. Deeply disappointed, I acquiesced and proceeded to the pool deck to advise the passengers of the necessary change of plans.

An hour later we arrived at Union Island – totally unknown to me and the captain. Nevertheless, there was a large crescent shaped beach with a wide expanse of bushes and tall flowering trees on the perimeter. It was decided that I would lead a scouting party to check out the quality of the beach and select the best location for the landing of the tenders and the spot to set up the bar and barbeque equipment for our all-day beach party. As I set off for shore, I now really did feel like a modern day Captain Cook, checking the entire beach front for possible hostile natives. The beach was completely deserted, however, but clean and welcoming - as was the clear and tranquil sea, ideal for swimming and snorkeling. Soon, an invasion of excited passengers swarmed the island, followed by crew members ready to prepare a feast of hamburgers, hot dogs and grilled fish. The unscheduled day on Union Island was quickly becoming a major hit for both the Realtors and the *Neptune* crew. Late in the day we saw our first island resident, an elderly, worn gentleman arriving at the end of the beach in a small fishing boat. I noticed that a number of our people had walked down the beach to talk to him and learn more about our unscheduled destination.

A few minutes later, Ralph Prichard, the president of the association, rushed back to inform me of the fisherman's warning that we should stay away from the bushes and trees lining the beach. "The sap is quite poisonous," he said, "and can cause serious blisters on the skin. Worse, it has been known to cause blindness if it gets into the eyes." Just as he finished the warning, Bob Cook, the association director and my client, approached me to ask if he could return to the ship. His eyes were very red and painful and his vision blurry. At the same moment, I noticed his goggles and mask attached to a branch of a tree he had cut to keep his wet snorkeling equipment off the sand. The very poisonous sap had obviously transferred from the goggles to his eyes. When I realized this I could hardly breathe, as I immediately assumed the worst. The sun was setting as we quickly cleared the beach and tendered back to the ship. A concerned staff was attending to Bob, who secured in his cabin, was moaning in pain and indicating he could no longer see.

After a number of calls to emergency agencies on the nearby islands, it was decided that we would forgo the next planned stop in Grenada, and leave immediately for Barbados, one of the largest islands in the eastern Caribbean. Barbados had, most importantly; the best hospital trained in handling health emergencies resulting from poisonous sap, which we discovered was prevalent throughout the chain of islands we were visiting. That sleepless night was the most terrifying of my entire life. Each hour I went to check on our patient in his cabin, finding no change in his condition. In between, I prayed for Bob's recovery; cursed myself for planning the trip and for allowing us to land on Union. After working together for three years, Bob was not only my client, he was also a friend.

At the conclusion of the ten longest hours of my life, the *Neptune* docked at the Barbados pier at the same moment a brilliant morning sun rose. As I helped Bob to a waiting transfer to the hospital, I was encouraged to learn that the pain had subsided and there was a hint of blurred vision when he was able to open his eyelids. A police vehicle met as we disembarked, and with lights flashing, rushed us to the nearby hospital. To my great relief, less than an hour later, Bob exited from the emergency room with his sight restored, thanks to special medication the doctors had applied to his eyes. It really felt like a miracle.

And just when I thought things could not get any better, I learned that our cruise director had discovered a dental lab that could make false teeth on the spot. A few hours later, our single lady passenger arrived back on the *Neptune* more attractive than ever, with a flashing grin that reflected dentures she claimed fit better than her originals. Barbados, to this day, has had a special place in my heart.

Later that evening, our magical cruise continued leisurely back to our starting point, arriving in San Juan early Saturday morning after a perfect, relaxing day at sea and a joyful Final Night Banquet, complete with Greek dancing and the traditional riotous smashing of dinner plates.

As we entered the airport for our flight home, I don't think I have ever seen a more welcoming sight than that beautiful, gleaming Pan Am jet, waiting to take us home to Chicago. The passengers were on board, ready for take-off, to be followed by the ever popular open bar, as I walked to my seat in the last row. How excited I was to know I would soon be home to my new wife. That evening I could regale her with the tale of my week-long nightmare, knowing full well she would not believe a word of it, convinced I had really enjoyed a week sunbathing in the warmth of the sunny Caribbean while she endured yet another week of Chicago's cold and snowy winter.

As I sat watching my fellow-travelers enjoy those last hours of vacation, I breathed a massive sigh of relief, vowing, after my experiences of the last week, I would never sell or embark on a cruise ship again. Little did I realize at that moment I would indeed continue to sell and escort groups on cruises around the world. Even more unlikely, I would later travel frequently to Finland during the course of two years to refurbish a cruise vessel which I would subsequently manage as it cruised the Hawaiian Islands. Or, more unlikely still, that I would start a company that would develop and install cruise software systems to the industry world-wide. Most ironic of all, however, would be finding me one evening in Athens telling this tale to the owners of the same Epirotiki Cruise Lines during dinner after selling them our software some two decades after surviving the cruise from hell!

Travel - Expecting the Unexpected

The world is a book, and people
who do not travel only read one page!

SPENDING MORE THAN THREE decades of my working career designing, selling and operating travel programs worldwide, there would bound to be many memorable moments. Three such experiences have earned their own chapters; *Iwo Jima, The Cruise from Hell,* and *the Pope and Pasta.* In this chapter, I'd like to offer a series of vignettes that provided me with indelible memories, and confirmed just how different people react to unusual circumstances.

Never Underestimate a Lawyer

"There's a World Expo next year in Osaka," I advised my boss at International Travel Service. "Let's design and sell a series of back-to-back charters to Asia." With Steve Martin's approval, a total of six charters were negotiated with Northwest Airlines, departing between May and September 1970.

In those days airline charters could only be sold to "affinity" organizations and all the seats could only be purchased by members and their families. Our initial departure was offered to the Chicago Bar Association, and all 164 seats sold out within a few days of the announcement early in the year.

And why not! It was an exceptional value – a two week trip including round-trip air fare to Asia on a Northwest 707 airplane, deluxe hotel accommodations at the new Imperial Hotel in Tokyo, the Miyako Hotel in Kyoto and the famed Peninsula Hotel in Hong Kong; all sightseeing, many lunches and two dinners at the cost per guest of $899.00!

The charter departed Chicago in mid-May (A few months prior to my July 4th marriage.) and I was the host and guide. Thankfully, the entire trip was a great success, and our return flight from Hong Kong to Chicago was loaded with 164 very happy passengers and literally tons of electronic bargains and tailor-made clothing purchased in the then best outlet mall in the world – Hong Kong.

Our flight plan called for a stopover in Tokyo for refueling. Upon arrival we were informed that the ground crew had discovered a mechanical problem with our 707 aircraft, and we were being transferred to a brand new 747 that only recently had begun service between Tokyo and Seattle. With more than 350 seats now available for our 164 guests and the opportunity to fly the newest and greatest aircraft in the world, there was joy and excitement among our lawyers as the 747 ascended gracefully above the vast Pacific toward Seattle and ultimately Chicago – a most pleasant surprise ending to the trip. That is, until some three uneventful hours into the flight when passengers on the right side of the aircraft yelled "fire," followed by a very loud bang with the aircraft suddenly listing to the right.

"This is your captain speaking. As some of you may have noticed out your window, one of our engines did catch fire, but it was quickly extinguished. You can be assured, however that the engine has now been shut down for safety reasons. There is no need for concern, as these new planes have a redundancy of power and can continue to fly with our three operating engines."

Following this rather heart-stopping event and announcement from the cockpit, we all sat back to enjoy our comfortable, spacious accommodations – until some minutes later when another explosion and fire on the left side of the aircraft had passengers in a true panic mode.

"This is your captain again. We have had to shut down engine number three as well. But not to worry as this new jet can continue to operate with two operating engines. We have just past the midpoint across the Pacific, and will be making an emergency landing in Anchorage. While it will be necessary to slow our speed, we will hopefully arrive there in just under three hours from now."

As I surveyed the aircraft I could not help but notice that the fear and concern for my own life was now clearly shared by my fellow passengers. A few minutes later I saw members of the Chicago Bar trip committee standing huddled together near one of the exit doors. Assuming that they were praying together (as so many appeared to be doing), I approached to discover they were discussing, somewhat heatedly, whether the special group life insurance policy purchased by the association for our charted flight would apply if we went down into the Pacific on this crippled 747 instead of our originally chartered 707. At that moment, I knew everything would be fine – and the world could never have enough wise and focused lawyers.

Just as the sun was rising over the Anchorage Airport, our 747 limped slowly toward the runway, aglow with the flashing lights of the fire and rescue equipment. I was the first off the aircraft to meet with Northwest Airlines managers to review plans for our ultimate safe return home to Chicago.

The good news was that a 707 was waiting to whisk us there once passengers cleared U.S. Customs and Immigration. The bad news, upon arriving at the departure gate, was being greeted by our new aircraft, a totally grey fuselage of a 707 without a single drop of paint on it and no indication of its ownership. As you might expect, this was met with shock, skepticism and a definite hesitation to board on the part of all, including our illustrious committee, who took it upon themselves to again discuss the validity of the insurance policy if we flew our last eventful leg on a nameless, naked aircraft.

Assured by Northwest that this was indeed a safe, new aircraft that had not yet been painted in the company colors, a tired though reluctant group of world travelers, with a story to tell, and a committee of relieved lawyers with no insurance claims to process, headed home.

THE HIGHEST PRAISE – TEXAS STYLE

The vibrant city of Hong Kong was the setting for another career highlight and memorable moment in the fall of 1986. It started the summer before when Winnie and I hosted a group of U. S. Association Executives on a study mission to the Chinese colony. The main purpose of that trip was to visit mainland China, which had only a few months earlier opened its border to Westerners for the first time in decades.

During a reception at the Peninsula Hotel, I saw Bob Burns, a hotel executive I had worked with when he was CEO of the Hawaiian Regent Hotel in Honolulu. I had heard he had been recruited by a Chinese tycoon to oversee the design and construction of what would be the most deluxe hotel in Asia, and destined to be acknowledged as one of the top hotels in the world during the late 80's. The next afternoon, Bob arranged a hard hat tour for our group, culminating with a Champagne toast on what would be the top floor of the new Regent, with a view overlooking the famed Hong Kong harbor.

"I have a client I believe could be talked into offering the Regent as their top dealer travel award next fall if the price is right," I mentioned to Bob during our second glass of champagne. By the time we left the construction site the deal was done; Coleman Company's top dealers would be the very first group to enjoy this magnificent hotel.

Following a soft opening in late summer of 1986, eliciting glowing reviews, this masterpiece was now prepared to welcome their first major incentive program with 200 Coleman dealers arriving each week during the entire month of October.

Traveling a few days prior to the first group's arrival, I met with the Regent management team to finalize the accommodations and activities to be provided for our guests. On my first tour of the property I was truly awed by what I saw, and especially the magnificent three-story lobby with its floor to ceiling windows offering a 180 degree uninterrupted view of Hong Kong's incredible harbor. The large guest rooms, also overlooking the harbor, would set the standard for future five-star hotels as they featured bathrooms with soaking tubs and separate glass showers that continue to be a feature today at Four Seasons and other top rated hotel chains around the world.

After this initial walk through, I feared that the Coleman dealers would not appreciate such opulence. Now, you need to understand that dealers earned this trip by selling heating and air conditioning units for campers and mobile homes throughout the Midwest and South. Thanks to the Coleman Company and the annual incentive travel awards, the dealers were well-traveled but not terribly sophisticated. And the initial group of 200 guests would be from the great state of Texas – the ladies with the bouffant hairdo and gaudy costume jewelry, and the men with their cowboy boots and Stetson hats.

Those very dealers arrived the next morning, bedraggled and exhausted from their eighteen hours of travel from Dallas on Singapore Airlines. Bob Burns, his top management team and I were in the lobby to meet this motley crew. Up to this moment, the creator of the "Best New Hotel in the World" was likely expecting a parade of New York banking types, arriving in their tailored suits and wearing Rolex watches. Instead, through the glass doors arrived the very best that the Coleman Company had to offer.

It culminated with one oversized Texan who stopped directly in front of Mr. Burns and his team, looked out over the vast marble lobby to the breath-taking view beyond, tipped his hat and taking the toothpick out of his mouth, declared in a booming voice with a proper Texas drawl, "This is the best God damn motel I ever saw!"

The looks on the faces of the Regent management team was priceless!

Over the years, as Bob Burns hosted presidents, statesmen, celebrities, and billionaires from all over the world, I wondered how often he re-told the story of the hotel's most unusual praise form a most memorable guest.

Oops

Some of the nicest people I escorted in the late 70's were farmers and their families from the Midwest. My relationship with the American Farm Bureau included coordinating their annual convention in Honolulu one winter, and another winter planning a special Caribbean cruise following the annual Farm Bureau meeting in Atlantic City in mid-January.

The best definition for the word "desolate" would be a cold and windy Atlantic City in January, so a relaxing week-long cruise was quite appealing to the membership from the Illinois and Iowa state bureaus. We had chartered Epirotiki Lines 300-passenger *Jupiter* out of San Juan, and two Pan Am 707s to transport our guests from Chicago and Des Moines to Atlantic City and then on to San Juan following the convention.

Because there was no terminal at Atlantic City (just a runway and a small, private aircraft hangar), we carefully planned the Pan Am flight schedule insuring that the two aircraft landed at least an hour apart, as there were just enough school buses in the city to transfer the passengers from only one plane to their hotel on the Boardwalk. Therefore, it was a great surprise to me, as I awaited the first flight, to look up and see both aircraft flying nose to tail, and landing one after the other at exactly the same time. This unexpected incident quickly demonstrated just how nice these farmers really were, as half the group waited almost an hour without complaint and in reasonably good humor in the cold for those few school buses to return and transfer them to their hotel. Our continuing Pan Am flights to San Juan a few days later were right on schedule and our passengers arrived in good form to embark the *Jupiter* for seven relaxing, warm and sunny days in the Caribbean.

Upon the ship's return to San Juan, our happy and tanned guests boarded the two 707s, ready to return to face the bitter winter months on their Illinois and Iowa farms. A few hours later the Pan Am charters landed in Chicago and Des Moines respectively. Traveling with the Illinois contingent I awaited the delivery of the luggage at baggage claim at O'Hare Airport. As the bags started to arrive, I noticed that no one was picking up any of the luggage. Finally, I started looking at the luggage tags. Strange – all the addresses indicated small cities and towns in rural Iowa. Being an "astute" escort, I quickly realized that Pan Am in San Juan had loaded the Chicago bound aircraft with the Des Moines bound luggage and vice versa.

Given the small towns and hamlets throughout two of the largest states in the Midwest, it took Pan Am weeks and at great cost to complete the delivery process. As experts listed the many reasons for Pan Am's ultimate demise some years later, I somehow felt this costly mistake could easily be added to the list.

SO, WHERE THE HELL ARE THEY?

"Instead of a traditional cocktail party at the hotel before our group dinner, would it be possible to have host families invite them into their homes for a real Irish experience."

"A grand idea. Let's do it, and I will help arrange it myself." replied the 71 year old Mayor of Galway, Bridie O'Flaherty.

It was spring of 1986 and I was on a planning visit with my good friend and local tour operator, Brian Moore, arranging a five night incentive trip for some 800 Coleman dealers to Ireland's beautiful west coast with visits to Galway and Killarney. As most incentive trips from the U.S. tended to visit the capital of Dublin, the mayor and management of the Great Southern Hotel in Galway were most excited about our plan and were eager to show our guests that Galway was, indeed, the "best city," and determined to make it the highlight of their Irish visit.

To accommodate such large numbers of Coleman dealers, we planned to operate four separate groups of 200 travelers back-to-back in late fall of that year. And following a late night of dining and Guinness with Bridie a unique "Meet the Irish" evening was finalized. Vans filled with 20 guests would be transported to selected Irish homes in various Galway neighborhoods. The local families would then be provided with funds to purchase Irish Whiskey, Guinness and other beverages for a one-hour cocktail party for their American visitors before their return to the hotel for a gala buffet dinner.

Six months later Brian and I met the initial group as they arrived in Galway. We were somewhat anxious, but confident – given the warm nature of the Irish – that our somewhat unusual plan of local hosted parties would be as much fun as we had expected. It was the excess of fun that was unexpected.

The vans departed the Great Southern Hotel at 7:00pm for the hour long visits, with the anticipated return by 8:30pm for the group dinner at the hotel.

At 8:30, Brian, the Mayor and I sat in the ballroom awaiting our hopefully happy travelers and the stories they would tell of their evening with the 'locals.' An hour later our lonely trio plus an anxious kitchen and wait staff started to wonder and worry – where the hell are they? (This was life before mobile phones and instantaneous communications.) By 10:00 there was disbelief and overcooked food in the kitchen, when the sound of very lively, happy travelers arriving, along with, unbeknownst to us, their uninvited host families as well as assorted local neighbors who had joined the fun at host's homes to welcome the Americans.

So instead of our 200 Coleman Dealers returning at 8:30 for dinner, now after 10:00pm, we had more than 300 "Yanks" and "locals" who in two and a half hours became great friends, caring less about the cold tables of food on the buffet, instead wanting to continue the party. And party they did – well past midnight!

Having worked on so many incentive trips in countries around the world, I remember sitting there amazed at the scene and thinking how different nationalities could be. This event was quite typical of the gregarious and incredibly friendly Irish. If I had arranged a similar event in Switzerland, our same travelers would have had pleasant visits with their reserved hosts, and then be back for dinner no later than 8:29pm.

At the end of that wild and unexpected evening, a tired but smiling Mayor came over to give me a good night peck on the cheek and told me it had been years since she had so much fun. "Bring more Yanks next year!"

The Pope and Pasta

"**I** MUST INFORM YOU, YOUNG man, that His Holiness will not be addressing your guests this July. He will have just completed a grueling, emotional visit to his homeland and we plan to move him directly from Warsaw to Castel Gandolfo for necessary rest and recovery."

This rather direct and stern rejection was presented to me in the Papal Office of the Vatican by an ancient, clearly disinterested Cardinal responsible for Pope John Paul II's official schedule.

"But just last week Archbishop Hickey assured me this meeting with the Serrans had been definitely set up and the purpose of my meeting with you today was to finalize the arrangements," was my feeble attempt to argue my case to an obvious set of deaf ears.

This disappointing visit to the Vatican in late January, 1985 started six months earlier when our company was appointed the official travel coordinator for Serra International's 25th Global Convention in Rome. Our responsibilities included the coordination of air transportation and hotel accommodations for some 2500 members world-wide. Originally, this Catholic lay group was founded to encourage and financially assist young men entering the seminary preparing to dedicate their lives as priests throughout the Americas and Europe.

I had committed to Archbishop Hickey, the spiritual leader of Serra, that, as president of Group Travel Unlimited, I would set up all arrangements and personally lead a group of escorts and guides during the five day convention the first week of July the following year. Six months later, having now spent four cold and damp January days finalizing hotels, bus shuttles, as well as high masses with Vatican-based cardinals in each of the four major basilicas in the Eternal City, my final assignment had been to work with the Papal Assistant to set up Pope John Paul's appearance and remarks at a gala final banquet at the Cavalieri Hilton Hotel on July 5th – the spiritual highlight of the convention.

As I walked dejectedly back to my room at the Excelsior Hotel, it also occurred to me that not only did the convention just lose the major reason for traveling to Rome for their 25th conference, I also would not be celebrating my own 15th wedding anniversary with Winnie this year on July 4th, as I will be stuck here in Rome – without her or the Pope.

Following a much needed glass of wine at the hotel bar, I went to my room and made a phone call to the Chancery Office in Washington, DC to leave the "bad news" message for the Archbishop. To my surprise, I was immediately connected with the prelate who asked for the details of my recent conversation. After listening intently, he inquired when I was leaving Rome, and then asked if I could remain through the next day. Early the next morning, I received a message that another meeting with the same irritable Cardinal had been arranged for late morning. Arriving with some trepidation, I was lead into the same office to confront the same red-clad gentleman who was now a smiling, congenial "old soul" who advised that the Pontiff would indeed be available to meet with the Serrans after all. However, since the Pope would need to be brought to the Vatican by helicopter from Castel Gandolfo, would it be acceptable to me and the Serrans to adjust the schedule for a private daytime visit in the Audience Hall on July 4th at midday. I could not say "yes" fast enough.

Once the arranged audience was finalized, the Cardinal took my hand and gently asked that I share the Holy Father's message of warmest greetings to his friend, the Archbishop, and to assure him that nothing is more important to the Pontiff than encouraging young men to join the priesthood which is so critical to Christ's Church around the world.

Victory! Now what to do about my 15th wedding anniversary… Ironically, it was not Cardinals or Archbishops that saved the day, but two nuns, Sisters of St. Joseph, my younger sisters, Maureen and Betty. As both were teachers and had free time during the summer, they became willing babysitters, allowing me to recruit Winnie as an escort for the convention in July – with the opportunity to sneak away on the fourth for a quiet anniversary meal in one of our favorite cities.

Following the Serrans arrival in Rome, arrangements proceeded smoothly, with the delegates enjoying the daily planned activities while awaiting the highlight – their private Papal Audience. As dawn broke on July 4th, it could not have been a more perfect day. And the excitement was palpable as the Serrans awaited entry to the Audience Hall late that morning. The ushers were careful to lead us into the Hall with ample space between each row to allow Pope John Paul II to walk down each aisle for a personal interaction with all invited guests. The applause was deafening as the Pope, together with Archbishop Hickey, entered the Hall. And after a short welcome, John Paul extended his personal appreciation for the important work of all in attendance. He then proceeded to walk down the aisles to shake hands and extend his blessing to all attendees. For any Catholic such a close encounter with a Pope is memorable. It was even more impressive with an energetic John Paul II, clearly in the prime of his papacy, his powerful features enhanced with a warm and winning smile making a lasting impression on everyone in attendance.

With the convention now a success, it was time for Winnie and I to enjoy the remainder of our anniversary day. After the very busy last few days, it started in true Italian style - with a traditional afternoon siesta. Refreshed and relaxed we headed out in the evening for that special anniversary meal.

Previously, I had asked our local travel service provider for a recommendation that was not a famous Roman restaurant or a popular tourist spot, but a quiet trattoria frequented by the locals. He knew just the spot and offered to make a reservation for us.

When we arrived at Ristorante San Ignazio as the sun was setting, it was clear the maitre d' had been advised of our anniversary. After a warm greeting, he led us to a prime table offering an incredible view of the small but incredibly beautiful Piazza of San Ignazio, with the imposing façade of the famous Jesuit Church directly in front of us. It was like dining in a Hollywood designed stage set – almost too perfect to be real.

Moments later a bottle of wine was delivered, but no menus. While we sipped the wine, a waiter arrived with two plates of pasta – somewhat unexpected, but appreciated. What was also unexpected was just how incredibly delicious this first treat was! Sitting there, on a perfect Roman summer evening, with the lights flickering in the piazza buildings and a hum of Italians quietly enjoying their meals, we seemed to be part of a romantic Roman movie. Soon, another smiling waiter arrived bearing two more plates of pasta, even better than the first. This was enthusiastically devoured while we waited for the menus – which never came. Instead, yet another bowl of enticing goodies arrived – creating a culinary ecstasy for a couple of Americans that could not be happier.

By this time a few hours had passed and a second bottle of wine appeared while the maitre d' made some suggestions for our "Main." Although we thought we were full, our perfectly cooked Mediterranean Sea Bass and tender Veal Chop were so delicious there was not a morsel left on either plate. Finally bidding *arrivederci* to the great staff, who together with the setting and the wonderful food provided us the most memorable anniversary, we knew we had just experienced what would be the best anniversary dinner we would have in our 48 years of celebrations.

As we arrived back at our top floor suite at the Excelsior Hotel, I exclaimed, "This anniversary has been perfect! In fact the only thing missing is the fireworks display that Chicago and Washington had offered in our honor the last fourteen years."

The words had not left my lips when there was a loud "boom" and the dark sky was suddenly full of bright colors. As we stepped out on our balcony, we were treated to our anniversary fireworks – Roman style.

July 4, 1985 – a special day for us, thanks to an accommodating Pope and a perfect meal in a setting only Rome could provide.

THE RIGHT TURN AT NAPA

HOW FORTUNATE I WAS. I loved my job, and I felt I was quite good at it.

Being President of GTU (Group Travel Unlimited) did require working long hours and traveling too much, but I was well-compensated for my efforts. I was responsible for a staff of 170 in three offices, stretching from Washington, D.C. to Honolulu, along with the more than 50,000 travelers who used our services each year to attend conventions and meetings around the globe. In fact, GTU was the nation's largest and best known meeting coordinator among the leading U.S. associations and corporations.

There were excellent "perks" that also went with the job. As GTU was the largest customer of both United and American Airlines, I flew First Class, making my extensive travel schedule less stressful. The company was also the largest supplier to the top resorts throughout the Hawaiian Islands, so my frequent visits there featured suite accommodations in the finest hotels. Our family even benefited by enjoying annual vacations at the top resorts of the Hawaiian Islands. So, in a word, life was good!

GTU was actually owned by Bob McGregor, a crafty Scotsman, who also owned the largest tour operation in Hawaii. Our relationship was excellent, as he was a "hands off" owner, thus providing GTU autonomy in day-to-day operations. Being a good Scotsman, however, and getting up in years, he could not resist a generous offer by the Carlson Company to acquire GTU in the spring of 1985. The Carlson executives who were negotiating the purchase indicated that GTU would operate as an independent division within their travel conglomerate with no anticipated changes to our current operation.

Once the sale was completed, Carlson assigned a Chief Financial Officer to help me with our division budgets and accounting. Bob Buser was an experienced financial manager who had worked within Carlson for years, and was pleased to transfer from the Minneapolis headquarters to Alexandria, Virginia. In turn, I looked forward to the insight and advice from someone who knew the inner workings of the parent company.

Shortly after his arrival, we spent a morning on our next twelve month budget. At the end of the meeting, he looked at me and said, "You should know that within a year you will be a different person."

"What do you mean?" I replied.

"Well," he explained, "the company owners are ruthless, heartless and will sacrifice anything for the bottom line. I guess that is why they are the second largest private company in America according to *Forbes*." Although taken aback, I assured Bob that they would not change me or my attitude toward our employees and clients. And, thankfully, we would continue to operate a long way from the Minneapolis headquarters where most of the other divisions resided.

The next few months went well during the "honeymoon" period, and I must admit I found it intriguing being part of such a diversified organization that included, in addition to other travel divisions, the Radisson Hotel chain, Regent Cruises and even TGI Friday's restaurants. My initial concerns developed when the CEO and his team visited our office to welcome the GTU staff to the Carlson Company, and assured them of job security, better benefits and a brighter future for our division. Immediately after his speech, during a short walk to lunch, he asked me how many of the existing staff could we now cut to improve the bottom line.

As the year went on the pressure and challenges of working for Carlson increased. The monthly budget meetings with all division presidents were brutal. Some of my colleagues who had been beaten up for years described the sessions as being a defendant on trial in a hostile courtroom every thirty days. They were right; it tended to be a nasty experience. If you made your numbers that month, home office executives wanted more. If you missed your budget projections, God forbid! Additional stress was created when internal consultants arrived to "advise" our experienced GTU managers on how to "better do their job," without ever attempting to understand why we operated the way we did. This caused rumors to spread that our senior managers would soon be replaced with people from the home office. To make matter worse, our division was transferred to work under a vice president who had originally fought against the acquisition of GTU, and who considered our division a threat to his domain. Company politics at its worst!

Early spring of the following year, I needed to get away from the office for a long weekend with Winnie, who also needed a break, as my now long hours at work, including weekends, gave her full responsibility for our three young children. A relaxing visit to northern California was planned. Just prior to our departure for San Francisco, we learned that it had been raining constantly there for more than a week, and more rain was in the forecast. That forecast was accurate as it was pouring when we checked into the Meadowood Resort in Napa Valley. We were advised that the Napa River was flooding its banks, so our planned wine tasting at various vineyards was out of the question. In fact, if we needed something from the nearby town of St. Helena, we were advised to get it right away as the rest of the valley would be flooded by the end of the day, making travel only possible in a rowboat. We purchased a few bottles of locally produced red wine and a few books in the drenched shopping area, and settled in for a rainy few days in our luxurious, but somewhat isolated hide-away retreat.

That afternoon, halfway through our first bottle of Cabernet, Winnie turned to me and said,"I think I really do not like you very much anymore. You are not the same person you used to be. Even your children are not crazy about you either."

It was one of the very few times in my life that I was speechless. Once I was able to communicate, we began a long and serious discussion on how my job with the new company was changing how I was now relating to my own family, friends and employees. As we moved on to the second bottle, the damaging "cause and effect" of this change in personality became evident to both of us.

That night we enjoyed yet another bottle while having an unusual dinner in the resort's restaurant. Since no one could enter or leave Meadowood due to the three feet of water covering Route 29 and the entrance to the resort, the few stranded guests were joined by the chef, cooks, wait staff and all other employees for a candle lit (there was no electricity) buffet dinner. By the end of the evening, Winnie and I agreed that I needed to resign, even though I had no immediate plans for employment. It was a relief, and somehow we knew it was the right decision, and things would work out.

The next morning, bright and early, I called my boss to advise him of my resignation. When he asked why I had made such an unexpected decision, I simply said, "To get back the quality of my life."

Later that morning, the sun came out, the river receded, and we decided to drive south to a drier Monterey resort where we completed our weekend relaxed and excited about our uncertain future.

I agreed to remain with GTU for an additional two months to provide Carlson sufficient time to find my replacement. During that time, Winnie and I decided I should start my own company, confident that some loyal clients and employees would, in time, find me.

A second mortgage on our home provided sufficient collateral for a bank loan to start Discovery Meeting and Incentives. Initially operating out of our home's den, the early days were a real family affair. Soon we found a townhouse in Old Town Alexandria to serve as Discovery's first real office. Thankfully, the company did grow, both in size and profitability, and became the firm foundation for a career that took many unexpected turns leading to new directions during the remainder of my working days. (Don't worry; you will be subjected to a few of those stories in future chapters.)

Throughout it all, however, I never forgot the two most valuable life lessons learned that fateful day in Napa. Working hard to make a good living and enhance one's family wealth is a virtuous goal, but not at the expense of one's quality of life. And, as importantly, ALWAYS listen to your wife!

VEAL MONTEREY

THE CANDLES ON THE dining room table flickered, casting a warm shadow on our guests. My choice of music enhanced the atmosphere without disturbing the enjoyable conversation as the six of us feasted on one of Winnie's delectable meals in our Belle Haven home.

"This is absolutely delicious," Carol exclaimed enthusiastically. "What is it?"

"It is called Veal Monterey," Winnie explained. "It's a recipe I found from that restaurant in Highland Park we were talking about last week."

"Veal Monterey" softly repeated Carol's husband, Jim, almost to himself. Then he turned to me and asked if I had ever heard of the S.S. *Monterey*.

"Last I heard, it was rusting at a pier in the Bay Area since being retired from service by Matson Lines more than a decade ago." With my response, I had no idea I had just stepped on a veritable land mine – one that would dramatically affect my life and that of my family for the next three years. It would be a true career changer, thanks to a simple veal dish served during a leisurely neighborhood dinner in the fall of 1986.

I had never met the Kurtzes prior to that evening. Winnie and Carol had become acquainted at the neighborhood swimming club, talking while their six children were dive bombing each other in the pool. We had much in common since Jim and Carol had moved to the Alexandria area from the North Shore of Chicago just as we had. So, at the end of the summer season Winnie thought it would be fun to invite them to our home for dinner. How could she have known then she was also inviting the "God Damn Boat," as she fondly called the *Monterey*, into her life?

I had a follow-up meeting with Jim a few weeks later, and he explained the value of the *Monterey* due to the antiquated U.S. Jones Act. Once the ship was refurbished, this law would allow the ship to operate throughout the U.S. waters of the Hawaiian Islands with limited competition. In fact, he had already signed a purchase agreement with the union that currently owned the ship, and planned to restore the vessel as a deluxe cruise ship offering seven-day cruises in paradise. All he needed to achieve this ambitious goal was to raise $16,800,000 through a limited partnership he had recently set up.

"I understand you have had a lot of experience working in Hawaii. You could be very helpful to my project if you would agree to assist by providing the marketing data required to sell partnership units." Jim stated.

"While the project sounds interesting, I do have my own incentive travel company which keeps me busy full time," I countered, thinking my response would end the conversation.

Soon, I learned that one of Jim's strongest attributes was persistence, and the more I thought about the possibilities of the project, the more interested I became. A few weeks later, I was providing marketing data and copy, as well as producing a marketing video to sell the concept to potential investors. Soon after that, I was hooked!

I found myself traveling around the country, making presentations to prospective investor groups, and meeting with some success. The challenge, however, was a deadline defined in the prospectus requiring the full sixteen million to be in the bank within a three month timeframe. Going right down to the deadline, the final million was committed by the Bechtel Family Foundation in San Francisco, with a major stipulation requiring, in turn, a commitment from me as well. The terms of their investment stated that I agreed to stay with the project as the Chief Operating Officer. As we celebrated at a chic San Francisco restaurant that evening, I pondered what this new turn of events would mean for me. What have I gotten myself into? Turns out, I had no idea!

Once the partnership was official, the *Monterey* was towed to a Tacoma shipyard to conform to a Jones Act requirement that all steel modifications must be completed in the U.S. This work included the addition of sponsons at the waterline on both the port and starboard sides of the vessel. The design would assure stability when new cabins were added during the more extensive rebuilding effort in Finland by the main contractor, Wartsila.

At the same time, it was now my responsibility to staff Aloha Pacific Cruises, the partnership entity that would market, sell and operate the S.S. *Monterey* once the refurbishment was complete. These activities included hiring a nationwide sales team, setting up a reservation center and selecting an advertising agency – all with the focus of selling a dream vacation on an elegant, historic cruise ship sailing the beautiful islands of Hawaii.

In late November 1987, the *Monterey*, with the necessary steel work completed, left Tacoma under tow for the Wartsila shipbuilding yard in Helsinki, where the real rebuilding and refurbishment would begin. Two weeks later we received a frantic call from Wartsila advising that the tug and *Monterey* had encountered a severe winter storm in the Atlantic south of England, and had parted ways. Without power, it was feared the ship would drift until overtaken by twenty-foot waves and 80-mile an hour winds, and ultimately sink - joining the numerous pirate ships and naval vessels lost in the same way over the centuries. And with its demise a multi-million dollar project would be brought to an unexpected and inglorious end. For two days we held our collective breaths and feared the worst. On the third morning we rejoiced at the good news; the tug regained control after a fierce struggle, and was continuing into the Baltic Sea. In retrospect, the good news was in reality an omen of the challenges ahead.

In late January, the *Monterey* was sitting snuggly in a shipbuilding berth at Wartsila's Helsinki yard. With great enthusiasm, Jim Kurtz and I flew to Finland for the first of numerous visits during the next year and a half during the renovation effort.

Now, if you have ever thought of visiting Finland during the winter – don't! Daylight arrives around noon and is gone by 2:00pm. That's right, twenty-two hours of darkness – and it is freezing cold.

Further, if you have ever considered working and negotiating with Finns – don't! They are tough as nails, and stubborn as mules. I did admire, however, that they work hard and they play hard. With a project of this magnitude, which the company apparently underestimated during the bidding process, day-long meetings turned into shouting matches, followed by a long, hot and miserable sauna with the Wartsila executives to "calm the nerves." This was followed by drinking vodka before, during and after a long dinner. It was their clever way of winning the war. The Finns were used to this battle plan; we were usually hung over.

While the battles continued, thankfully so did the refurbishment. Our team at Aloha Pacific Cruises became genuinely excited and confident about the project and the *Monterey's* future. There was so much interest in the return of the beloved ship to the Hawaiian Islands, our planned Inaugural Voyage from Copenhagen to New York was sold out a year in advance, adding revenues of more than two million dollars to the coffers. We were now truly on our way!

Two months prior to the delivery, however, a serious problem arose. During the initial sea trails in early spring, the U.S. Coast Guard officials sent to Finland by the U.S. government to monitor the work being done by Wartsila, discovered a major design flaw. During a life boat drill at sea, it was discovered that when the life boats were lowered to the water, they tipped over upon reaching the sponsons that extended from the sides of the vessel. The Coast Guard did not take kindly to this "glitch," and required that the sponsons be modified. OK, so modify the sponsons. Not so fast – to maintain its Jones Act status as a U.S. flagged ship any work on the steel frame could only be done in a U.S. yard.

A relatively minor repair in Finland would now become a major disaster. In reality, it would mark the beginning of the end for the "God Damn Boat."

To begin with, the long-anticipated maiden voyage was canceled and those critical two million dollars of payments would be refunded. Further, the vessel would then sail empty to the U.S. where the necessary sponson repairs could be done at a yard in Baltimore. The crew hired early in the spring was housed in a Baltimore hotel and trained while the ship was in dry dock. All the while, our available funds were fleeing from the partnership's bank accounts.

Finally, the first passengers embarked from Baltimore during a warm summer night, and headed south through the Panama Canal destined for the glorious "Homecoming" celebration in the *Monterey's* original home port of San Francisco.

Along this inaugural journey we had planned visits to several U.S. ports on both coasts– each memorable stops where impressive crowds of travel executives and local press waited to tour the vessel before its ultimate arrival at its new home in Hawaii. In its heyday the *Monterey* was known to cater to movie celebrities. For our one-day visit to Los Angeles we hired a few aging stars, well past their prime – Margaret Sullivan, Chad Everett, and scraping the bottom of the celebrity barrel, we even invited Zsa Zsa Gabor to join the fun. And a great party it was.

The real celebration, however, came two days later, with its triumphant, nostalgic arrival in San Francisco – the *Monterey's* final visit before heading to Hawaii. Here we pulled out all the stops. The mayor, other politicians and celebrities attended a shipboard gala cocktail party. The result was advertising that you could not buy – with full page features in all the newspapers and live TV coverage of the visit in all the major cities on the West Coast, our prime audience for Hawaii cruising.

We now had reason to be excited and enthusiastic about the future. We had put the challenges and problems of the past two years behind us. It was now smooth sailing ahead for the famed vessel and Aloha Pacific Cruises.

It was a sunny crisp morning as the S.S. *Monterey* prepared for a triumphal departure from San Francisco's Pier 35. Hundreds of friends, family and press filled the pier. Streamers floated down from the decks where the excited departing passengers waved, and a band played. Winnie and I stood watching the ship, now such an important part of our lives, slowly pull away from the pier, headed out into the bay. We both felt relief now that the worst was behind us.

There she was, a floating reminder of a glorious past, and now a proud new entry in the ever-growing fleet of cruise ships worldwide. A vessel with 500 guests filled with anticipation of the week-long trans-Pacific cruise ahead.

With a young and enthusiastic crew of two hundred attractive college graduates looking forward to an adventure in Paradise before facing the real world.

A renowned chef now facing the biggest challenge of his young life.

An ice carver who would arrive in Hawaii in the ship's brig to be turned over to the local police for attempting bodily harm to a fellow crew members.

A mentally unbalanced Staff Captain who six months later would be sending letters threatening me and my family.

Yes, the next leg of my history with the ship had begun. As I celebrated, at that special moment, reflecting on all that the *Monterey* and I had achieved, I could not possibly have imagined the "fun" had just begun!

Monterey Postscript

While the SS *Monterey* departed San Francisco in a blaze of nostalgic glory and five days later her maiden arrival in Hawaii to a shower of confetti and leis, a brass band and hundreds of well wishers at the dock, the reality was a vessel financially limping to her new home at Honolulu's Aloha Tower. The significant revenue loss due to the cancelled Trans Atlantic Inaugural cruise and the extensive repair work in the Baltimore shipyard had taken its toll. Miraculously, the ship continued to offer week long cruises for almost a year. However, each week the financial challenges became more intense. Early winter of the following year there were serious discussions with Cunard Line and the Hyatt Hotel chain to purchase and operate the vessel within the rigid requirements of the Jones Act. I remember a final meeting in New York where the Hyatt Chief Financial Officer expressed to me amazement that a million dollar enterprise was being financed weekly "out of a cigar box."

Once those negotiations could not be finalized, there was no choice but to suspend operations awaiting a sale by Wartsila, holder of the prime mortgage.

Several months later the sad ship was purchased by a small start up cruise company in Naples and successfully cruised the Mediterranean for a good number of years.

As part of my compensation with Aloha Pacific Cruises, I continued to own the reservation and on board software initially developed by my partner, John Fraser, and his team during the *Monterey's* return to service. In 1990 we discovered that there was a need for our software by smaller and start up cruise companies that could not afford to develop their own internal systems. Out of the ashes rose a new Discovery Travel Systems, marketing and supporting "Cruise Partner" and "Ship Partner" solutions to cruise lines around the world. Ironically, one of our initial clients was

American Hawaii Cruise, the very aggressive competition to the *Monterey* during the year it operated in Hawaii.

Perhaps even more ironic was that small Italian cruise company who purchased the *Monterey* for Mediterranean cruising was so successful it decided to build two new 4,000 passenger vessels. (It is now the largest cruise company in Europe with some 24 mega vessels.) To best support its growth it turned to (you guessed it!) Discovery Travel Systems. So, in the end, my initial involvement, as a result of that memorable Veal Monterey dinner served by Winnie years earlier came full circle providing a vibrant software business and ultimately the unexpected source for our retirement living here in Newport.

SS Monterey Cruising Hawaii

Iwo Jima

IN THE EARLY '90S a retired Marine colonel and I started a new division within World Travel Partners dedicated to providing tours and travel services for World War II veterans returning to the major battle sites in the Pacific for 50th anniversary remembrances. These tours would be spread out over four years, starting with a reunion in Guadalcanal in late fall of '92 through the final battle on Okinawa in June of '96.

Some, like the trip to Peleliu, were small in size but significant to those Americans who fought in one of the bloodiest campaigns of the entire war. Others were large celebrations, like the eight hundred veterans returning to be honored at the 50th anniversary of the "Liberation of Guam" during the summer of '93.

But the tour most veterans and our staff anxiously awaited was the one-day "Reunion of Honor" to the iconic island of Iwo Jima, scheduled for the third week of March, 1994. While this uninhabited, overgrown, almost inaccessible speck of land in the middle of the Pacific Ocean had been returned to the Japanese in 1968, for most Americans, Iwo continued to represent the grit, determination and bravery of the American soldiers that resulted in the Allies victory fifty years earlier.

So, it was not a surprise that six months prior to our special visit, Military Historical Tours had collected deposits for every one of the 1,200 seats on all four Continental Airline's DC10 aircraft scheduled for travel to the island on that historic day.

However, what we firmly believed would be the crowning achievement of Military Historical Tours quickly became a litany of mounting challenges that continued right up to and including the one-day visit itself. It started when the Japanese Self Defense forces who administer the island wanted no part in the visit by former American troops. While the U.S. government considered it a day of remembrance for all warriors from both countries, the Tokyo bureaucracy believed it would, instead, become a celebration of the American victory there. In spite of the ongoing deliberation between the military of both governments permission for the visit and memorial service continued to be blocked.

When word got out that the trip was in question due to the Japanese government's reluctance, Iwo veterans let their feelings be known. At one planning meeting the news of the Japanese position led a gruff, elderly Marine Sergeant to shout, "God damn it! We took Iwo once, and, if we have to, we'll take it again!"

Thankfully, another bloody battle was not necessary. With the continued pressure on the Japanese military and the personal intervention by the U.S. Ambassador to Japan, Walter Mondale, permission was begrudgingly granted for the day of remembrance. To make it as difficult as possible for the veterans, however, every visitor needed to apply for a Japanese visa – even though we were visiting an uninhabited island as a group for less than a day.

With the approval in hand the grand plans for the event continued to move forward. These included the participation of four former Commandants of Marine Corps as well as the actual induction of the new Commandant by the Secretary of the Navy on Mount Suribachi that afternoon. Additional guests for the memorial service included five Medal of Honor recipients, multiple starred generals from both countries, Ambassador Mondale, the wife of General Kuribashi, commander of the Japanese troops during the battle, and Joe Rosenthal, the photographer who took the most famous military photo of all time.

But the Japanese had yet another roadblock in hopes of scuttling the mission! Two weeks prior to our departure for the staging islands of Guam and Saipan, we received word that their military had declared that the existing runway on Iwo was not capable of accepting the weight of the DC 10s – with the added concern that there *may* be human remains of Japanese soldiers in *possible* caves under the runway itself that *could* possibly be disturbed. Although the evidence of officials at Continental Airlines countered this finding, the Japanese were adamant in the decision to not let the planes land. Even our own Department of Defense could not sway the Japanese decision, although fully suspecting the motivation behind it.

Thankfully, the President of Continental Air Micronesia (a former Marine) agreed to a major 48 hour adjustment to the airline's South Pacific/Asia route schedule to provide six 727s to replace the "overweight" DC 10s. Another obstacle was overcome, but for the Japanese bureaucracy, the battle was not yet over!

Prior to the official reunion on Iwo itself, the veterans were housed on Guam and Saipan, where they took local tours, enjoyed dinner parties and participated in memorial services while reuniting with old friends they served with during the war. It was a reunion of sorts for me, as well, reacquainting myself with many of the veterans I traveled with the previous two years.

March 21, 1995 – The big day finally arrived. Flight planning called for an initial departure at 7:00am sharp from both Guam and Saipan, followed by departures of the additional aircraft at fifteen minute intervals, with all six flights landing by 8:30am thereby allowing maximum time for the visit prior to the departure at dusk. I was on that first flight from Guam. We were boarded and ready to depart by 7:00am, except there was no sign of the three Japanese immigration officials assigned to process the visas while en route to Iwo. After a series of announcements, I finally left the aircraft and found them relaxing and enjoying coffee in the café, successfully ignoring the numerous requests for boarding. I rushed them to the aircraft, and we finally departed some twenty minutes behind schedule. This was critical for air control as six commercial aircraft were tightly scheduled to land where none had ever landed before.

As we approached the island, it was a clear and sunny morning. As a result, our destination was clearly visible - as were the other five 737s – all circling the island at the same time, and landing one immediately after the other, forming an aerial parade of honor to start the momentous day.

I was the first to disembark, and as I looked toward the hangers where the transport equipment was parked, I encountered an amazing sight. For the past two months two hundred and fifty young Marines from Okinawa had been tasked with clearing the original roads and paths to allow the trucks and vans to transport our guests around Iwo, including visits to the black sand beach and Mount Suribachi. Their work done, they now formed an honor guard from the aircraft to the hangers, standing at attention to welcome the arriving Marine heroes of another era.

Heading toward the line of smiling Marines, thunderous applause could be heard as the veterans, all who had waited a lifetime for this moment, walked through the long row to the constant refrain of "Welcome back, sir." The veterans, with tears in their eyes, returned the welcome with salutes. And so often their refrain, "It's so green!"

The veterans boarded the transports and were driven to the site selected for the memorial service prior to their individual day of exploration and reflection. Following the ceremony, one veteran with whom I had developed a friendship as a result of being together on a trip to Guam the previous year approached me.

"Are you planning to go down to the beach?" he asked.

"Yes, I was hoping to catch one of the first transports heading there."

"I know you must be very busy today, but I have something special I want do there and I would really like to share it with you, as you have been so good to me on these trips."

In our previous conversations, I had learned that after the war he returned to a small town in Michigan near Detroit, and worked for GM his entire career. He had lost his wife a few years ago and his only daughter was too ill to make the journey, so he was traveling alone.

We soon arrived at the beach, the site where more than 26,000 American causalities occurred, including 6,800 who had lost their lives so many years before. Today, the same beach was eerily peaceful, it seemed almost serene as he lead me to the spot he remembered landing with his buddies in the late afternoon that March day. Once there, he took out several pages of yellowed paper that had been carefully folded in the inside pocket of his jacket.

He then told me that a few months ago the children of his sister had cleaned out her belongings in the attic following her death, and had discovered a letter he had written to his parents while lying on this very beach that fateful night. Two of his friends on either side of him had been shot and killed before darkness descended, and he was convinced that it would be his turn when the fighting resumed after daybreak. That night would be his only chance to say goodbye to his family, by writing a farewell letter on that dark, lonely beach.

"I have not opened this since they gave it to me. Knowing that I was coming back, I wanted to read it for the first time right here where I wrote it. Thank you for sharing this special memory with me."

He proceeded to carefully open the aged papers, and with tears flowing, read aloud the details of the terrifying night, the loss of this two friends and expressing his own fear of impending death while thanking his family for the love they gave him growing up.

It was a special moment for both of us. And I could not help thinking of the thousands who landed with him who never had the same chance to write home. He and his fellow veterans were there today to remember them.

Following a warm and emotional embrace, I left him with his own thoughts as he again looked out on the Pacific, where the sun was now on the downward trajectory on its western slide toward Japan. After a few steps, I noticed a small memorial service breaking up further down the beach toward Suribachi.

And then that first note of a bugle stopped me in my tracks. That melody – both haunting and eloquent – from a single musical instrument was so familiar to me. From the playing of Taps during those Memorial Day services in my childhood following the war, to the same mesmerizing sound during the burial of President Kennedy that sad November day in Arlington, it was a melody that inevitably captures one's emotions.

But at that moment its meaning and eloquence took those emotions to a whole new level – "Day is Done."

I stood there silently, looking across the black sand where clusters of veterans and their families stood listening – some with heads bowed, others looking up to Mount Suribachi where the American flag once flew defiantly for the world to see. The only sound was a quiet splashing of the Pacific waves on the black stones, and the solemn sound of the bugle. I now knew that the year-long effort to make this a memorable and meaningful day for the veterans of Iwo Jima now spread across this memorable place was a success. At the same time, I realized that these same veterans provided me with a deeper understanding of the tragedy of war - and the courage of those who had to fight it. In the end they gave me one of the most memorable days of my life.

"All is well, safely rest, God is nigh"

ALL'S WELL THAT ENDS WELL

I HELD IN MY HANDS two long pieces of plain white cloth – my mother's going away to college gift, given to me the night before I was to leave for Georgetown. Since I was obviously bewildered by such an unusual present, she finally had to explain that these were her "apron strings," and I was now on my own.

This gift and declaration did not prevent her, however, from offering one final piece of advice, "You will be meeting and dating many young ladies while at Georgetown, but always remember you were brought up an Irish Catholic, so it would be best if you could find a nice Irish Catholic girl to marry."

Seven years later, I was living in Chicago and home in Massachusetts for the holidays. One night my mother looked at me and said, "Well, the girl doesn't actually have to be Irish, but it would still be best if she were a Catholic."

A few years later, during another Christmas visit, she said, "I don't care what she is – it's time for you to get married!" Mom really wanted grandchildren!

Little did she know that, at the time, I was actually dating a Catholic girl from Chicago. Karen worked at Pan Am, where I was a Sales Representative. She was quite attractive, with vivid red hair – and a personality to match. During that next spring and summer we dated quite regularly.

Using my Pan Am discounts, I arranged a trip to Europe that fall for my parents, plus aunt and uncle, and I planned to accompany them. Karen had decided to leave Pan Am and received the customary farewell discount ticket valid for 30 days. Since she had no travel plans, I asked her if she would like to join us for the last week of the trip. Being a typical naïve male, little did I realize I was sending a less than subtle message to both she and my mother of a marriage proposal likely happening while on the trip.

The family's grand European adventure was a great success, and my parents welcomed Karen when she joined us the last week in Germany. Unfortunately, it did not take long for me to discover the mistake I made in inviting her, as our previously pleasant relationship developed into a series of extended arguments centered on the misunderstanding I had inadvertently created. While I enjoyed her company, I had never seriously considered marriage. Part of the reason was her "my way or the highway" attitude that was always lurking right under the surface. Plus, I was not ready for such a major step. To be honest, I was really enjoying my bachelor life in Chicago.

And there was a further subliminal complication in the person of an actual Irish Catholic girl who also worked at Pan Am. While I had never gone out with Winnie Moran, I really liked her. She was always smiling and happy, and she made me feel good whenever we spoke at work or when we would run into each other at Butch McGuire's or the Lodge on weekend nights. In fact, it was Winnie, not Karen, who was the recipient of the cold, two-day old fried clams I brought back from the Cape that summer so that she could try my absolute favorite food in the world. Surely, Freud would have found something significant in that strange offering.

On a beautiful brisk Swiss autumn morning I knew I had come to a major crossroad in my life, and asked Karen to walk with me to a hill overlooking Lake Lucerne. We sat on the steps of a church and had a serious discussion that we should realistically have had months before. It was a most difficult conversation as I explained to her I had no intention of proposing to her on this trip or anytime in the future, and it would probably be best for both of us if we stopped seeing one another. It was an awful morning and made for a most difficult day and evening in the company of my confused parents. The following morning she left, as scheduled, to return home while my family and I continued on to Paris, our last stop of the whirlwind trip. While realizing I had disappointed both she and my mother, I knew that I had made the right turn at the crossroad, and now needed to focus on the road I had selected.

It was not long before I asked Winnie out on a real date, and, as expected, we really enjoyed each other's company. For the second date, however, I made the mistake of inviting her to join me at the theater. Having bought the cheapest seats, we were so far from the stage that we could barely see the performance or hear the music of Man of La Mancha. Worse yet, I was on a diet and had given up beer, ruining my otherwise bubbly personality. The night was an unmitigated disaster, and neither of us thought we would go out with each other again.

But the attraction was too strong, and soon we were spending the entire summer and fall dating. I was clearly winning her over with my adorable canary yellow Cutlass convertible! As time went on, I knew we were getting serious when I would give up a prime parking space near my downtown Chicago apartment to pick her up in her parents' "geographically undesirable" ethnic neighborhood on the north side.

The inevitable occurred late one evening during the annual early-December Pan Am Christmas party. During a slow dance, I looked at her lovingly and said, "Since my two sisters are teachers, it would have to be in the summer."

Without hesitation or batting an eye, her mind raced through the 1970 calendar she had memorized for just such an occasion and responded, "How about Saturday, July 4th?" Never had there been a more romantic proposal and acceptance.

Our wedding was on a beautiful July 4th in Chicago. In spite of my pre-marriage trepidation and nerves, the ceremony went off without a hitch, and the reception was a smashing success. I now had a companion and together we would move down that road I had chosen.

As with all roads, it had its hills and valleys. It also had its bumps along the way. Although the first six years living in the Lincoln Park area of Chicago were idyllic as we waited for our first child to join us. Soon thereafter (and I mean soon) there were two more, and we were now a real family moving down that same road.

Taking a new job and moving to Alexandria, Virginia, those bumps sometimes became pot holes. I was constantly traveling around the globe for my work, while Winnie was too often a "single mother" responsible for the children, our home and those continual basketball, soccer, football, baseball and lacrosse practices and games. There were times she even suggested we stop the car on the road so she could get out and leave me with the children - permanently. Nevertheless, through those challenging times, we always found the time to communicate – often during a late night dinner after the children were in bed and the day's work done.

I also earned some valuable points during those difficult years by graciously accepting Winnie's aged mother, with a weak heart and dementia, into our home when the doctor indicated she had only six months to live. And I remained gracious during the entire four years she was with us.

And then there was the "God Damn Boat," which totally engulfed our lives for three long years. But Winnie could not completely fault me on this as she was partially responsible for this unexpected challenging project due to her serving that Veal Monterey!

As the journey continued, we all too quickly found ourselves "empty nesters," as our children moved out to encounter their own crossroads. Fortunately our road led us to our retirement home in Newport. Realizing that including the words "smooth road" and "Newport" in the same sentence is an oxymoron, it has been exactly that. It got even better when we sold our software company and my first assignment was to fire the accountant and human resources manager. Winnie, who held these jobs for many years, was thrilled! And it got better yet when I retired a year later, providing more time for us to do whatever we want to do – together. In a way, it seems much like "Back to the Future" and those idyllic first years of marriage in Lincoln Park.

It is hard to believe that more than forty-eight years have passed since the right turn at my personal crossroad that day in Switzerland. Never, for a second, have I regretted the decision that I made that day, or, more importantly, the proposal I subsequently made to Winnie the next year. I cherish each day I now spend with her.

I love the trips to Europe, Hawaii and other wonderful vacations we now enjoy. But, most of all, I like our evenings together in our cozy Newport home when she will make a delicious meal, which we enjoy with wine, candlelight, music and good conversation. Ending each evening on a "high" I imagine few couples could understand.

I have never looked back to speculate what my life would have been like if my decision had been different at that crossroad in Lucerne. Nor have I ever speculated about life with any of the other girls I dated in high school or college. There is simply no reason to do so.

I thank God every day for that right turn made so long ago. There is no one else I could have spent my life with, no one I would rather spend every day with now, no one I could ever love more than Winnie, my wife - and best friend.

Epilogue

Breaking the Mold

This epilogue is the result of another topic suggested for our Write-Life course. One week the topic was, "Something unique or special about your family," and a beautiful little two year old granddaughter then living in Chicago came to mind. What better way to describe exactly how "breaking the mold" was impacting our lives than a personal letter to McKenna. At the time little did I realize that she would be able to read it without help three short years later when she turned five!

Dear McKenna;

It is hard for Gigi and I to believe you will soon be celebrating your second birthday. You are growing so fast and becoming so smart, so quickly. I have decided that this would be a good time to write my first letter to you and tell you about family, and, in particular, your mother's side of the ever growing family in which you play such an important role. One in which you broke the mold.

Throughout history, families have been the back bone of all societies. Some are very large and others quite small. A dominant characteristic, however, has been the sharing of a common nationality, even as recent generations migrated from all over the world to a welcoming America. As an example, when Gigi and I came into the world, like you did almost two years ago, we each became part of large Irish American Catholic families whose heritage evolved in the poor but beautiful country of Ireland. While it was my grandparents who moved to this country, Gigi's parents were directly from the Old Sod. In those days it was expected that the many nationalities in America would remain true to the cultures they left behind. It was a common belief that you "marry your own kind." In fact, it was my own mother's final piece of advice as I left to go to college that "It would be best if I married a good Irish Catholic girl." Ten years later, I did marry my Irish Catholic girl – your grandmother, Gigi. And together we had three Irish children, your mother and your uncles, Kyle and Conor (or as you fondly call him, CaCa).

Oh, what a nice traditional Irish family we were, and continued to be until our Keelin met your father. Now Roberto was Catholic, but certainly (with his parents originally from the Dominican Republic and Haiti) not Irish. Philippe was not an Irish name, and he definitely did not look Irish.

As your parents started to date, Gigi took an immediate liking to your father. Part of the bond was that they were both Loyola Chicago Ramblers – still reliving that miracle 1963 NCAA basketball victory, while lamenting the fact that it would never happen again in either of their lifetimes. Now, to be honest, I was not as excited about their dating, but it really had nothing to do with the fact that your father was not Irish. As a proud father, my concern was that Roberto would not be good enough for my perfect daughter. Soon he won me over, and I began to question whether Keelin would be good enough for him! As it turned out, I had nothing to fear as they were – and are - perfect for each other.

Two years later, their union created a wondrous little girl they named McKenna, who had a blend of Irish, Dominican and Haitian genes, clearly breaking the traditional Irish mold. Thrilled with their initial success in parenting, they are now planning to provide you with your own sister or brother this summer.

As we now watch you quickly develop your own special personality, I think of how fortunate you are. It is clear your parents are providing you the love, discipline and freedom to let you grow, and aspire to whatever you wish to be and do in the many years ahead. And to be able to do it in a society today that embraces the diversity of the cultures you represent. One where you are respected for who you are, for your accomplishments and for the special relationships you develop with those who come into your life.

Now, don't for a minute think it will be an easy journey. There will be times when you will not be very good, and your parents will not be happy with you. (In fact, your "terrible twos" must soon be endured by those loving parents.) When you are a teenager there will undoubtedly be times you hate your mother and think your father is dumb, but those will quickly pass and simply be bumps in the road.

Gigi and I have heard much about your father's family over the last few years. It is unfortunate that his parents will not have the same opportunity to watch you grow as Gigi and I are able to do. While dying much too young, they must have been wonderful people and great parents. You can be very proud of them for giving us your father and your Uncle Murat – even if he is a little crazy.

While you and your father have changed our traditional Irish family forever, there is more Broughan diversity on the way. Later this year Uncle Kyle is marrying Christine, whose parents migrated from the Philippines; so future cousins will add an Asian culture to the family. And just yesterday, Uncle CaCa and Aunt Leigh gave us Nora Ruth, your new cousin. Talk about culture shock – Leigh is not even Catholic and, stranger yet, she is from a most exotic place - the state of Maine!

So look at what you started. Our once homogeneous Irish Catholic family is being transformed into a wonderfully diverse multi-cultural collection of grandchildren for us to enjoy and spoil. How exciting it will be for you as your new brother or sister and cousins join you in the months and years ahead. They will be some of your best friends on your life's journey, just as your own parents are with your aunts and uncles today. That's what families are all about.

While our time with you may be brief (as we enjoy the seventh or eighth inning of life), we plan to savor every minute with each of you. We realize how fortunate we are, knowing how interesting and exciting our ever expanding family is becoming, now made up of a mixture of ancestors from the distant island of Ireland to the sunny islands of the Dominican Republic and Haiti, on to the Philippine Islands in the far Pacific and back to that strange and wondrous home of moose and lobster – Maine.

I will close with a little secret that only the two of us can share. While I will love each of our grandchildren equally, you will always be very special, because you were the first to break the mold; and because you are a beautiful person, just like your mother and your two grandmothers.

Love,
Da

Now, five years later, the reality of our growing and diverse family continues enriching our lives. McKenna does have a brother, Brendan (my buddy), and four beautiful, loving cousins, Nora, Ayla, Winnie and Maeve, shown together in living color on the back cover of this memoir. Indeed the mold had been broken – and what a kaleidoscope of joy it has rendered!

REMEMBERING. . . .

My Mother and Father, Mary and John, who made so many sacrifices raising us during those early years.

And our dear sister, Betty, a special person who gave joy to so many – and left us too soon.

66238135R10073

Made in the USA
Middletown, DE
10 September 2019